A GUIDE TO
DICKENS' LONDON

DANIEL TYLER

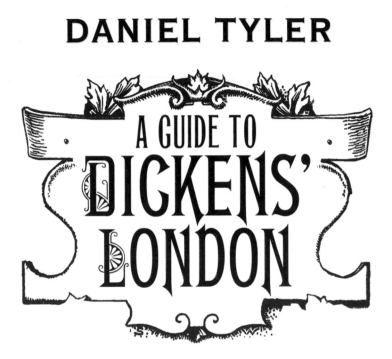

A GUIDE TO
DICKENS'
LONDON

HESPERUS

Published by Hesperus Press Limited
28 Mortimer Street, London, W1W 7RD
www.hesperuspress.com

First published by Hesperus Press Limited, 2012
© Daniel Tyler, 2012

Illustrations © Helen Chapman
Photography by Tom Miller
Cover image: A Balloon View of London, published by
Banks and Company, 1851/Guildhall Library, City of London/
The Bridgeman Art Library

Designed and typeset by Madeline Meckiffe
Printed in Jordan by Jordan National Press

ISBN: 978-1-84391-352-8

CONTENTS

INTRODUCTION

Charles Dickens was fascinated by London. It provides most of his novels with their main settings. His characters make their homes there, they find employment there, they cross its bridges, frequent its taverns, patronise its shops, attend its churches, and are locked up in its prisons. London's long and illustrious history could be seen everywhere about the city and it emerges into Dickens' pages. Nineteenth-century London was undergoing dramatic transformation on its way to becoming a truly great modern metropolis. In Dickens, the city found one of its greatest writers, and it did so during one of the most remarkable periods in its rich history.

Dickens lived for most of his life in London. His family moved there in 1823, when he was eleven, and even after he moved to Kent, in the last decade of his life, he continued to work at offices in the capital until his death in 1870. He had an obsession with walking through the city streets. He did so by day and by night, sometimes covering miles at a time. He built up a deep familiarity with the city that stirred his imagination and enlivened his writing. He once wrote of his need of London's streets and crowds, in order to make progress with his writing, which was virtually impossible when he was long absent: 'It seems as if they supplied something to my brain which, when busy, it cannot bear to lose. For a week or fortnight I can write prodigiously in a retired place, a day in London setting and starting me up again. But the toil and labour of writing day after day without that magic lantern is immense!'[1] His daughter Kate later explained that London proved a necessary resource for her father's creative pursuits: 'he would walk through the busy, noisy streets, which would act on him like a tonic and enable him to take up with new vigour the flagging interest of his story and breathe new life into its pages.'[2]

Dickens paced the streets when he was writing his fiction, needing the change of scene and the stimulation of other people, but in doing so he was replaying over and over the many other occasions when he had walked the same routes. Some of these occasions had been deeply disturbing. He was for a long time haunted by a humiliating episode working in Warren's Blacking Factory as a boy. At this time he would walk daily from his lodgings in Camden Town and then in Southwark into central London, to Hungerford Stairs, near the Strand. He would sometimes head to London Bridge and look across at St Paul's before his daily work began. When his marriage very publicly broke down in the late 1850s, he found consolation, or at least diversion, in walking again through the city, this time from his house near Russell Square. No doubt the streets became ever more deeply associated with the events of his own life. David Copperfield once went to London, we are told, 'to lose myself in the swarm of life there'. If that was Dickens' aim on his frequent walks, he may have found that, instead, the London streets reminded him how impossible it was to lose himself, to step outside his own personal circumstances.

Certainly, in Dickens' fiction, London resonates with his experiences in the city, as well as those of his characters and with its own history. It stirred Dickens' creativity in innumerable ways. This book explores the places that meant most to him and examines his often vibrantly imaginative responses to them. It looks at the way that London took on a newly stimulating life in his fiction. It considers those places in the city that Dickens returned to again and again, whether on foot or in print.

ABBREVIATIONS

Quotations from the novels are taken from the Oxford World's Classics editions and chapter references are given in the text. I have used the Penguin editions of *Sketches by Boz*, *Pictures from Italy* and the *Selected Journalism*. Other references are given in the endnotes.

The following abbreviations have also been used.

PP	The Pickwick Papers
OT	Oliver Twist
NN	Nicholas Nickleby
OCS	The Old Curiosity Shop
MC	Martin Chuzzlewit
CB	Christmas Books
DS	Dombey and Son
DC	David Copperfield
BH	Bleak House
LD	Little Dorrit
GE	Great Expectations
OMF	Our Mutual Friend
ED	The Mystery of Edwin Drood
SB	Sketches by Boz
MHC	Master Humphrey's Clock
PI	Pictures from Italy
UT	The Uncommercial Traveller
SJ	Selected Journalism
AF	Autobiographical Fragment
Letters	The Letters of Charles Dickens, 12 vols, eds. Storey, Tillotson, House (1963–2002)

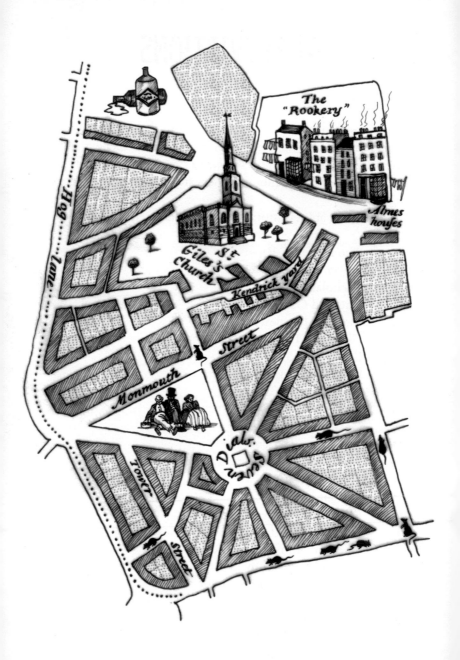

LONDON'S SLUMS

Dickens' imagination was consistently drawn to the slum areas of London. The booming population of the British capital in the nineteenth century had created overcrowding on an unprecedented scale. The city was ridden with slums, or 'rookeries', in areas such as St Giles, Jacob's Island in Bermondsey, and Agar Town.[1] Many commentators and campaigners drew attention to the appalling conditions in these areas, and Dickens' fiction played an important part in publicising these horrors. In many of his works, Dickens considers the injustice of their existence in close proximity to more well-to-do districts, critiquing the inequalities of the city. He adds his distinctive voice to those calling for the problem of urban housing to be addressed and what emerges is the vigorous social critique for which he is known.

In his earliest works, however, including *Sketches by Boz* (1836), a series of short papers on London life, the vehement social criticism bubbles under the surface, and Dickens rarely allows it to come out in full force. Instead, he revels in the creative potential and the anarchic energies of the bustling, densely packed, high-spirited, chaotic slum areas. These sketches are often curtailed before the unruly energy of the pauper crowds can erupt into vehement life, but they contain much of the vitality and potential that would soon be given vent in Dickens' longer fiction.

ST GILES

The abundant and varied life in the slums is evident in the description of St Giles in an early sketch entitled 'Gin Shops' (1835). In this sketch, written when Dickens was twenty-two, the narrator heads for a drinking establishment in the vicinity of Meux's brewery, which was in St Giles, on the corner of

Oxford Street and Tottenham Court Road. St Giles had long been one of the most derelict and impoverished areas of London. It fascinated Dickens, as John Forster noted in his biography. The squalor and depravity found in its narrow streets had already been memorably depicted by artists such as William Hogarth in the eighteenth century. It was not until the 1840s that anything changed in the living conditions there. The slum clearance projects that attended the construction of new roads, such as New Oxford Street in 1847, began to clear out the area – although much of the slum remained until the building of Shaftesbury Avenue and Charing Cross Road in the 1880s.[2] Today, the old church of St Giles still stands, but the brewery and the slums are long gone.

In his sketch, Dickens' account details the inhuman conditions into which many of the urban poor were crammed:

> The filthy and miserable appearance of this part of London can hardly be imagined by those (and there are many such) who have not witnessed it. Wretched houses with broken windows patched with rags and paper: every room let out to a different family and in many instances to two or even three; fruit and 'sweet-stuff' manufacturers in the cellars, barbers and red-herring vendors in the front parlours, and cobblers in the back; a bird-fancier in the first floor, three families on the second, starvation in the attics, Irishmen in the passage; a 'musician' in the front kitchen, and a charwoman and five hungry children in the back one – filth every where – a gutter before the houses and a drain behind them – clothes drying and slops emptying from the windows: girls of fourteen or fifteen with matted hair walking about barefooted, and in white great-coats, almost their only covering; boys of all ages, in coats of all sizes and no coats at all; men and women, in every variety of scanty and dirty apparel, lounging, scolding, drinking, smoking, squabbling, fighting, and swearing. ('Gin Shops', *SB*)

The full and exuberant prose shows the scene teeming with life. The list of violent verbs at the end stretches the syntax to near breaking point and reminds us of the crowded, uncontrollable character of St Giles. At the same time, the description offers a taxonomy of the slum that threatens to tidy away the unruly, messy, crowded conditions into an orderly prose ('a bird-fancier in the first floor, three families on the second', etc.), like someone putting things away into drawers. It reveals a second impulse alongside the representation of the overcrowding and messiness of St Giles, one where Dickens can subdue the chaos by the power of his pen.

But if Dickens' description is able both to represent the disorder and to tidy it away, his response to the slum is equally torn between comedy and pathos. The passage shows Dickens' alert perception of the social problems posed by the unwholesome, detestable living conditions of London's slums and some compassion for those unfortunate enough to have to live there. But he does not develop extended sympathetic portrayals of, for example, the 'girls of fourteen or fifteen with matted hair walking about barefooted'. The poignancy of these cameos is held in check by the imaginative relish with which he sets about describing the grim conditions and the eruption of the sort of unruly life he was about to celebrate in his first novel, *The Pickwick Papers* (1836–7). The rapidity of the survey in this brief sketch speeds over the saddening details. The rhetorical devices are quick and subtle – as when his list of occupants of the slum tenements includes 'starvation in the attics', a sudden personification that is both humorous and appalled. The word musician is comically held in inverted commas, questioning the accuracy of the epithet, but without pausing to make any more of it before he identifies the occupants crammed into the next room.

While the exuberant rapidity of Dickens' descriptive prose sometimes skips past the horrors of the St Giles slum, on other occasions the writing registers the grim details. The reference to 'boys of all ages in coats of all sizes' is playfully rhythmic, but that rhythm is brought up short by the awful reality, 'and no coats at all'. In this early description of St Giles, the prose merges the sympathetic and indignant perspective of the social reformer with the imaginative and anarchic vision of the comic writer. It was to become characteristic of Dickens' early writing about London.

SEVEN DIALS

One area within the St Giles slums that entranced Dickens was Seven Dials, near Covent Garden. The area was originally established in the 1690s and featured seven roads converging at a single junction, then, as now, marked with a sundial pillar (though the pillar had been removed in Dickens' day and has now been replaced by a more modern variant). The intention behind this unusual construction was to maximise the number of houses that could be built there, but in the 1830s overcrowding had contributed to make it one of London's most dismal slums, part of the St Giles 'rookery'. Dickens found the location so compelling that he devoted one of his early sketches to it. His fascination was sparked not only by the bustling and unruly life in Seven Dials that provided material for his sketch but by its unusual topography. He wrote with mock grandeur that a first encounter with Seven Dials invoked feelings comparable to those of Giovanni Battista Belzoni, the explorer of Egyptian antiquities and the first man to penetrate the second Pyramid of Giza:

> The stranger who finds himself in 'The Dials' for the first time, and stands Belzoni-like, at the entrance of seven obscure passages, uncertain which to take, will see enough around him to keep his curiosity and attention awake for no inconsiderable time. ('Seven Dials', *SB*)

The awe inspired by an encounter with Seven Dials may be comically overstated, but Dickens' own 'curiosity and attention' is nevertheless awakened by the slum and his imagined stranger is diverted from any set purpose by the vibrant, miscellaneous life that surrounds him:

> The peculiar character of these streets, and the close resemblance each one bears to its neighbour, by no means tends to decrease the bewilderment in which the unexperienced wayfarer through 'the Dials' finds himself involved. He traverses streets of dirty, straggling houses, with now and then an unexpected court composed of buildings as ill-proportioned and deformed as the half-naked children that wallow in the kennels. Here and there, a little dark chandler's shop, with a cracked bell hung up behind the door to announce the entrance of a customer, or betray the presence of some young gentleman in whom a passion for shop tills has developed itself at an early age: others, as if for support,

against some handsome lofty building, which usurps the place of a low dingy public-house; long rows of broken and patched windows expose plants that may have flourished when 'the Dials' were built, in vessels as dirty as 'the Dials' themselves; and shops for the purchase of rags, bones, old iron, and kitchen-stuff, vie in cleanliness with the bird-fanciers and rabbit-dealers, which one might fancy so many arks, but for the irresistible conviction that no bird in its proper senses, who was permitted to leave one of them, would ever come back again. Brokers' shops, which would seem to have been established by humane individuals, as refuges for destitute bugs, interspersed with announce-ments of day-schools, penny theatres, petition-writers, mangles, and music for balls or routs, complete the 'still life' of the subject; and dirty men, filthy women, squalid children, fluttering shuttlecocks, noisy battledores, reeking pipes, bad fruit, more than doubtful oysters, attenuated cats, depressed dogs, and anatomical fowls, are its cheerful accompaniments. ('Seven Dials', *SB*)

For Dickens, 'the Dials' are full of imaginative potential. His prose bristles with enjoyment at the vibrancy of these streets. His writing is wilfully imaginative, despite the bracing realities of the place: he proposes lively analogies that attempt to reclaim the rag-and-bone shops as 'so many arks' and the brokers' shops as 'refuges for destitute bugs'. Even the disturbing analogy between the 'ill-proportioned and deformed' buildings and the children that live in them has imaginative vitality as an early example of Dickens' habit of anthropomorphising buildings in his writing, giving them the features of people, and enabling them almost to become characters themselves.

Seven Dials is most fully a place of potential for Dickens because of its distinctive topography. He starts the sketch with a stranger at the Dials about to move on, 'at the entrance of seven obscure passages, uncertain which to take'. It was a characteristic of Dickens' early novels that he did not begin them with a plotline in mind, but a meandering and digressive story would emerge naturally from a productive combination of characters and circumstances. The Seven Dials slum provided a representative instance of this combination, although the characters in his account were not yet fully developed. It had all the lowlife and intrigue that a novel such as *Oliver Twist* would extend into a complete story and it had a sense of latent possibility in the image of the wayfarer standing at the entrance to seven streets. The scene threatens to turn into a longer fiction when, later in the sketch, the 'still life' trembles into animation:

> Now any body who passed through the Dials on a hot summer's evening, and saw the different women of the house gossiping on the steps, would be apt to think that all was harmony among them, and that a more primitive set of people than the native Diallers could not be imagined. Alas! the man in the shop illtreats his family; the carpet-beater extends his professional pursuits to his wife; the one-pair front has an undying feud with the two-pair front, in consequence of the two-pair front persisting in dancing over his (the one-pair front's) head, when he and his family have retired for the night; the two-pair back *will* interfere with the front kitchen's children; the Irishman comes home drunk every other night, and attacks every body; and the one-pair back screams at every thing. Animosities spring up between floor and floor; the very cellar asserts his equality. Mrs A. 'smacks' Mrs B.'s child, for 'making faces'. Mrs B. forthwith throws cold water over Mrs A.'s child for 'calling names'. The husbands are embroiled – the quarrel becomes general – an assault is the consequence, and a police-officer the result. ('Seven Dials', *SB*)

The energy of these slum scenes is such that they persistently threaten to spring into violent life. It is as if they are waiting for the novelist that Dickens was about to become to release them into longer life. In sketches such as these, however, he does not allow them to get off the ground. Much academic commentary has argued that Victorian fiction unwittingly operates like the police in controlling the society it depicts, endorsing correct actions and attitudes, and clamping down on unacceptable behaviour.[3] In Dickens' sketch, the parallel is more knowing than this, as the work of the police officer is aligned with that of the writer, who brings a swift end to the unruly action by refusing to allow the anarchic plot energies to erupt into a longer narrative. Dickens does not yet turn the slum-dwellers into characters that could sustain a longer fiction. Instead, he limits himself to an impressionistic report of the dispute between archetypes: 'Mrs A.' and 'Mrs B.'. The quarrel 'becomes general' because in this way it has always been only general.

FAGIN'S LAIR (FIELD LANE)

In the novels that Dickens would go on to write, the characters that live in London's slums are described as named individuals rather than types. This is already apparent in his second completed novel, *Oliver Twist* (1838), where the street urchins that return each night to Fagin's lair play a prominent part in the fiction. Fagin's den is located near Saffron Hill, to this day a street in Camden, and off the adjacent Field Lane, which has since disappeared. We are given a description of the scene as Fagin skulks and shuffles through the back streets of Snow Hill:

> Near to the spot on which Snow Hill and Holborn Hill meet, there opens, upon the right hand as you come out of the city, a narrow and dismal alley leading to Saffron Hill. In its filthy shops are exposed for sale huge bunches of second-hand silk handkerchiefs of all sizes and patterns — for here reside the traders who purchase them from pickpockets. Hundreds of these handkerchiefs hang dangling from pegs outside the windows, or flaunting from the door-posts; and the shelves within are piled with them. Confined as the limits of Field Lane are, it has its barber, its coffee-shop, its beer-shop, and its fried-fish warehouse. It is a commercial colony of itself, the emporium of petty larceny, visited at early morning and setting-in of dusk by silent

merchants, who traffic in dark back-parlours, and go as strangely as they come. Here the clothesman, the shoe-vamper, and the rag-merchant display their goods as sign-boards to the petty thief; and stores of old iron and bones, and heaps of mildewy fragments of woollen-stuff and linen, rust and rot in the grimy cellars. (*OT*, 26)

Dickens writes with precision about the actual location of the slum, but it is also imaginatively re-envisioned through his prose. He describes a 'commercial colony' that is a burgeoning centre of trade, but the term 'colony' distances this illegitimate subterranean economy from the capital of the empire. The filthy and dismal conditions are effectively placed at odds with the natural land-scapes remembered by the place names, 'Saffron Hill' and 'Field Lane'. The 'huge bunches' in the shops turn out to be not flowers but handkerchiefs. The description contributes to the unfolding story in a way that was never the case with the sketches because it activates hints of an inevitable demise and the possibility of hanging. The handkerchiefs that 'hang dangling' in the street provide an image that invokes the threat of hanging that suffuses the novel and that is fearfully portended for Oliver, until, in one of the novel's several twists, it is Bill Sikes who meets that end.

JACOB'S ISLAND, SOUTHWARK

The site of Sikes's accidental hanging is Jacob's Island, another slum that Dickens describes evocatively and locates precisely. Jacob's Island was a miserably poor area of London, on the banks of the Thames, a little way downriver of St Mary's, Rotherhithe. Its gradual clearance in the nineteenth century was propelled by the notoriety that *Oliver Twist* had given it. The slum was at that time approached, Dickens tells us, through a narrow maze of squalid streets:

In such a neighbourhood, beyond Dockhead in the Borough of Southwark, stands Jacob's Island, surrounded by a muddy ditch, six or eight feet deep and fifteen or twenty wide when the tide is in, once called

Mill Pond, but known in these days as Folly Ditch. It is a creek or inlet from the Thames, and can always be filled at high water by opening the sluices at the Lead Mills from which it took its old name. At such times, a stranger, looking from one of the wooden bridges thrown across it at Mill-lane, will see the inhabitants of the houses on either side lowering from their back doors and windows, buckets, pails, domestic utensils of all kinds, in which to haul the water up; and, when his eye is turned from these operations to the houses themselves, his utmost astonishment will be excited by the scene before him. Crazy wooden galleries common to the backs of half-a-dozen houses, with holes from which to look upon the slime beneath; windows broken and patched, with poles thrust out on which to dry the linen that is never there; rooms so small, so filthy, so confined, that the air would seem too tainted even for the dirt and squalor which they shelter; wooden chambers thrusting themselves out above the mud and threatening to fall into it — as some have done; dirt-besmeared walls and decaying foundations; every repulsive lineament of poverty, every loathsome indication of filth, rot, and garbage; — all these ornament the banks of Folly Ditch. (*OT,* 50)

This is a forceful piece of writing of a scene that comprises a suitable backdrop to Sikes's demise because it makes visible the moral filth of his life. John Reed has suggested that Dickens' description of Jacob's Island has an accuracy that brings it close to plain reportage.[4] He locates the power of the account in its placing within a plot-driven narrative. There is much beyond this that invigorates Dickens' writing, however, including the fact that much of it is written from the perspective of a stranger, so that the scene is overlaid with his 'utmost astonishment'. The observation that there are 'poles thrust out on which to dry the linen that is never there' may not be strictly accurate according to some contemporary photographs but it nonetheless deftly represents the oddity of the scene and perceives at once both what is and what ought to be, in this slum area. When the verb in 'poles thrust out' is made active in 'chambers thrusting themselves out', it is as if the scene has taken on a personal life of its own and the buildings have become pushy, reminding us how readily sites in London themselves become characters in Dickens' novels. The word 'ornament' is well calculated as a final satirical thrust, as it implies a decorative capacity to the features described that is jarringly at odds with the reality that the features are barely functional, let alone ornamental.

At any rate, Dickens' description was sufficiently powerful to draw attention to the horrific conditions existing in this part of London. His account of Jacob's Island became the subject of a heated public controversy. Over a decade later, Dickens was astonished to learn that Sir Peter Laurie, an alderman of London whom Dickens had satirised in his earlier Christmas story, *The Chimes*, had denied the existence of Jacob's Island, supposing it to be the product of Dickens' imagination. Dickens responded immediately by adding a preface to the Cheap Edition of *Oliver Twist* exposing Laurie's mistake and asserting the need for social reform to begin by improving the living conditions of the poor. By 1867, the unwholesome conditions of Jacob's Island had been cleansed and Dickens noted in a new preface to *Oliver Twist* that year that the place was now 'improved and much changed'.

The controversy had propelled Dickens' writing about London's slums into the forefront of mid-Victorian investigations into the city's meanest living conditions. Working parties invited Dickens to address them concerning his knowledge of the slum areas. These experiences reinforced his understanding that his own fiction could make active interventions in the real world; and it nourished a perspective on London's slums – furthered in later novels – that recognised the injustice of their existence in a city where wealth abounded in close proximity. Much of Dickens' later writing about London's slums has a serious commitment to social reform. He increasingly considers (often implicitly) the possible contribution his writing could make to the cause of urban reform. He began to realise that his fiction could draw attention to the neediest areas, and that it had the capacity to rouse the interest and desire necessary for changes to take place.

STAGGS'S GARDENS, CAMDEN TOWN

In *Dombey and Son* (1846–8) Dickens wrote of another deprived area of London – the fictional Staggs's Gardens, located in the real Camden Town, an area where the Dickens family lived on more than one occasion. *Dombey and Son* is often understood to be the novel in which Dickens' later artistic maturity is first evident and so it is fitting that his writing about London's slums takes on a new importance in this novel.

The child, Paul Dombey, expresses a dying wish to see his first nurse, Polly Toodles. So his new nurse, Mrs Richards, takes him to her home in Staggs's Gardens. Dickens describes a settlement already torn apart by the railroad being built through it. The locals refuse to accept this development and believe their ragged tenements will outlast the interference:

> It was a little row of houses, with little squalid patches of ground before them, fenced off with old doors, barrel staves, scraps of tarpaulin, and dead bushes; with bottomless tin kettles and exhausted iron fenders, thrust into the gaps. Here, the Staggs's Gardeners trained scarlet beans, kept fowls and rabbits, erected rotten summer houses (one was an old boat), dried clothes, and smoked pipes. Some were of opinion that Staggs's Gardens derived its name from a deceased capitalist, one Mr. Staggs, who had built it for his delectation. Others, who had a natural taste for the country, held that it dated from those

rural times when the antlered herd, under the familiar denomination
of Staggses, had resorted to its shady precincts. Be this as it may,
Staggs's Gardens was regarded by its population as a sacred grove not
to be withered by railroads. (*DS*, 6)

Dickens writes fondly of the Staggs's Gardeners, who take a
pride in their dwellings and are adept at turning old things to
new uses. But their resourceful recycling takes them only so far
and this is an occasion when Dickens suggests that progress is
experienced not only gradually but also, sometimes,
catastrophically, as he writes about the arrival of the railroad
being like an earthquake wrecking the region. The coming age
of the railroad is already in his mind as he writes about the
ruinous slum. The 'old boat' may have been turned into a
summer house, but it will be rendered more antique by a
completely new mode of transport. The locals may be able to
'train' the plants in their gardens, but locomotive trains and the
age of the railroad would bring innovation and change in ways
that the Staggs's Gardeners could not imagine, and it would
transform their slums beyond recognition. Regarding their
tenements as a 'sacred grove' may have been an admirable fancy
and Dickens does not condemn them for their imaginative folly
– after all, it shares his own fondness for the country – but he
knew that the kind of imagination that resulted in real social
improvements, such as had arrived in Jacob's Island by 1867,
must not offer a retreat from deliberate action but should be
aligned with an active spirit of progress.

The return to Staggs's Gardens later in the novel constitutes a
rebuttal of its population's indulgent imagination:

There was no such place as Staggs's Gardens. It had vanished from the
earth. Where the old rotten summer-houses once had stood, palaces
now reared their heads, and granite columns of gigantic girth opened a
vista to the railway world beyond. The miserable waste ground, where
the refuse-matter had been heaped of yore, was swallowed up and gone;
and in its frowsy stead were tiers of warehouses, crammed with rich
goods and costly merchandise. The old by-streets now swarmed with
passengers and vehicles of every kind; the new streets that had stopped

disheartened in the mud and waggon–ruts, formed towns within themselves, originating wholesome comforts and conveniences belonging to themselves, and never tried nor thought of until they sprung into existence. Bridges that had led to nothing, led to villas, gardens, churches, healthy public walks. The carcasses of houses, and beginnings of new thoroughfares, had started off upon the line at steam's own speed, and shot away into the country in a monster train.

[...] But Staggs's Gardens had been cut up root and branch. Oh woe the day! when 'not a rood of English ground' – laid out in Staggs's Gardens – is secure! (*DS*, 15)

The railway transforms the region for the good. Dickens' description is favourable and on the side of progress. There is just a hint of menace in the account of the 'carcasses of houses' that were developed 'at steam's own speed, and shot away into the country in a monster train'. The image of a steam train is buried in this line about the sequence of houses, and it is not entirely positive. Whilst embodying technological and social advance, the train could also be fearfully destructive. The potential threat of the train, which Dickens later in the novel calls the 'monster of the iron road' and takes as an image of the 'remorseless monster, Death', is realised when the villain, Carker, is brutally run down on the railway.

Nevertheless, the coming of the railroad causes the derelict buildings of Staggs's Gardens to be replaced by new houses, better facilities and 'healthy public walks', and there are new opportunities for the former inhabitants. The last line of the quoted extract highlights the inadequacy of poetic fictions about the slums that resisted progress, such as those once held by the Staggs's Gardeners. Dickens' poetic allusion scrambles lines from Oliver Goldsmith and William Wordsworth. One of its effects is to undermine an unrealistic nostalgia that opposes change. The deprived area in *Dombey and Son* is enlisted in Dickens' thinking about urban development and, in particular, nineteenth–century progress, which gives his account here a deeper seriousness than his earlier writing about slums.

TOM-ALL-ALONE'S

In *Bleak House* (1853), the slum resides at the heart of the novel. It is the property at the centre of the Jarndyce and Jarndyce case and it is where Jo, the crossing sweep who is mysteriously connected to the events of the plot, lives. It is a major image in the novel for the nation's moral corruption, as Dickens frequently mentions in his descriptions of the slum the aristocrats and bureaucrats who do nothing to change it. But the slum is not only symbolic in the novel, as if it stands only for something other than itself, because it is also an instance of the squalid living conditions endured by many of the urban poor. Although it is not an actual site in London, it is representative of the slum areas that Dickens visited throughout the city, and of the conditions that he campaigned to have improved.

This is a novel that probes the links between different strata of society and between the different events that happen in a plot distributed across the social spectrum, as it asks 'what connection can there be?' In this vein, Dickens establishes connections in his writing between Tom-all-Alone's and the 'decent people' who live elsewhere. His thoughts about the slum are inflected by an indignation directed at those who could do something about the awful living conditions of their neighbours but choose not to. The slum takes an active part in the events of the novel later on. In the following passage, Dickens holds to account those who make speeches about Tom-all-Alone's but do nothing practical:

> Darkness rests upon Tom-all-Alone's. Dilating and dilating since the sun went down last night, it has gradually swelled until it fills every void in the place. For a time there were some dungeon lights burning, as the lamp of Life burns in Tom-all-Alone's, heavily, heavily, in the nauseous air, and winking – as that lamp, too, winks in Tom-all-Alone's – at many horrible things. But they are blotted out. The moon has eyed Tom with a dull cold stare, as admitting some puny emulation of herself in his desert region unfit for life and blasted by volcanic fires; but she has passed on, and is gone. The blackest nightmare in the infernal stables grazes on Tom-all-Alone's, and Tom is fast asleep.
>
> Much mighty speech-making there has been, both in and out of

Parliament, concerning Tom, and much wrathful disputation how Tom shall be got right. Whether he shall be put into the main road by constables, or by beadles, or by bell-ringing, or by force of figures, or by correct principles of taste, or by high church, or by low church, or by no church; whether he shall be set to splitting trusses of polemical straws with the crooked knife of his mind, or whether he shall be put to stone-breaking instead. In the midst of which dust and noise, there is but one thing perfectly clear, to wit, that Tom only may and can, or shall and will, be reclaimed according to somebody's theory but nobody's practice. And in the hopeful meantime, Tom goes to perdition head foremost in his old determined spirit.

But he has his revenge. Even the winds are his messengers, and they serve him in these hours of darkness. There is not a drop of Tom's corrupted blood but propagates infection and contagion somewhere. It shall pollute, this very night, the choice stream (in which chemists on analysis would find the genuine nobility) of a Norman house, and his Grace shall not be able to say Nay to the infamous alliance. There is not an atom of Tom's slime, not a cubic inch of any pestilential gas in which he lives, not one obscenity or degradation about him, not an ignorance, not a wickedness, not a brutality of his committing, but shall work its retribution, through every order of society, up to the proudest of the proud, and to the highest of the high. Verily, what with tainting, plundering, and spoiling, Tom has his revenge. (*BH*, 46)

The personification of the slum, encouraged by its unusual name, is part of Dickens' writing about it from the outset. The technique, whereby the slum is called 'Tom', anticipates the active part it will take, as if a character in its own right, in what turns out to be a sort of revenge plot. The disease that spreads in the pestilential air of the slum infects Jo, and then Charley and Esther, and probably contributes to Lady Dedlock's demise. While Dickens' early sketches treat slums as backdrops to potential action, in *Bleak House* the slum is one of the novel's most important motifs, it is at the centre of Dickens' strong social critique, and it becomes an active agent in the plot in its own right, as 'Tom' wreaks his revenge.

BLEEDING HEART YARD

In *Little Dorrit* (1857), Dickens' descriptions of the ramshackle dwellings of the working poor are compassed about with a similar set of interests: the burgeoning life that stimulates the novelist's imagination, the injustice of such conditions being allowed to exist, the possibility of redeeming the misery of the place with imaginative fancies, especially those prompted by its unusual name. In this case the name is particularly evocative: Bleeding Heart Yard. It refers to an area in Holborn still standing today, and which was one of the most impoverished, run-down areas of nineteenth-century London. Unlike the early sketches, this novel tells the story of some of the inhabitants of the slum.

Bleeding Heart Yard brings together the novel's characters: Arthur Clennam first goes there to visit the Plornishes, and so does Daniel Doyce, the optimistic factory owner with whom Clennam goes unsuccessfully into business later in the novel. Bleeding Heart Yard is also the scene of Pancks's industrious rent collecting for the patriarchal Mr Casby, so that the slum provides a point of connection in a novel that only gradually reveals hidden links between separate characters:

> As if the aspiring city had become puffed up in the very ground on which it stood, the ground had so risen about Bleeding Heart Yard that you got into it down a flight of steps which formed no part of the original approach, and got out of it by a low gateway into a maze of shabby streets, which went about and about, tortuously ascending to the level again. At this end of the Yard and over the gateway, was the factory of Daniel Doyce, often heavily beating like a bleeding heart of iron, with the clink of metal upon metal.
>
> The opinion of the Yard was divided respecting the derivation of its name. The more practical of its inmates abided by the tradition of a murder; the gentler and more imaginative inhabitants, including the whole of the tender sex, were loyal to the legend of a young lady of former times closely imprisoned in her chamber by a cruel father for remaining true to her own true love, and refusing to marry the suitor he chose for her. The legend related how that the young lady used to be seen up at her window behind the bars, murmuring a love-lorn song, of which the burden was, 'Bleeding Heart, Bleeding Heart, bleeding away,' until she died. It was objected by the murderous party that this Refrain was notoriously the invention of a tambour-worker, a spinster and romantic, still lodging in the Yard. But, forasmuch as all favourite legends must be associated with the affections, and as many more people fall in love than commit murder – which it may be hoped, howsoever bad we are, will continue unto the end of the world to be the dispensation under which we shall live – the Bleeding Heart, Bleeding Heart, bleeding away story, carried the day by a great majority. Neither party would listen to the antiquaries who delivered learned lectures in the neighbourhood, showing the Bleeding Heart to have been the heraldic cognizance of the old family to whom the property had once belonged. And, considering that the hour-glass they turned from year to year was filled with the earthiest and coarsest sand, the Bleeding Heart Yarders had reason enough for objecting to be despoiled of the one little golden grain of poetry that sparkled in it. (*LD*, I, 12)

The Staggs's Gardeners had been gratified by the imagined associations of the name of the place in which they lived. So too, the Bleeding Heart Yarders bring romance and poetry into their lives through the fanciful histories that they imagine for their Yard. Dickens pictures the local population as a cherished community. The slum is not the seat of vice and crime that he more typically imagined earlier on in his career and this is because it is now seen in the larger perspectives of the city's inequalities. Dickens is much exercised in this novel with satirising government bureaucracy in the guise of the infamous Circumlocution Office. The pauper inhabitants of Bleeding Heart Yard are delineated sympathetically as their circumstances are regarded as the symptoms of the gross inefficiencies of the Circumlocution Office. As with Tom-all-Alone's, the slum has come to represent national and governmental corruption in the eyes of the later Dickens. The imaginative vision he had of the slums in his early writing has given way to a more hard-edged confrontation with the realities of urban deprivation, and such imaginative fictions about the slums are the object of gentle satire in the later novels.

AFFLUENT LONDON

When Dickens was twelve, his father was incarcerated in the Marshalsea debtors' prison, and the young Dickens was sent to board in various lodging houses around London. John Dickens continued to find himself in financial straits, even after his release from the Marshalsea. In these early years, affluent areas of London – such as Harley Street, Cavendish Square, Grosvenor Square, Mayfair – could not have been further from Dickens' experience.

In his writing, affluent London is often seen to be outside Dickens' sphere of experience and its inhabitants are the targets of biting satire. He satirises the rich, and does so through their dwellings. In particular, he critiques the pride of the aspiring rich, who don the habits and the habitations of the wealthy, without being truly of their rank. And yet his writing is also sometimes tinged with a nagging sense of the injustice of his being shut out from these areas of privilege.

Nineteenth-century London contained many residential areas that were the exclusive haunts of the wealthy: areas such as Mayfair, squares such as Grosvenor and Cavendish. With the burgeoning of a professional and commercial class, some squares, such as Cadogan Place and Golden Square in Soho, were being vacated by the aristocracy and left to those with commercial interests. Dickens finds in these squares the opportunity to satirise social-climbers and over-reaching go-getters. He writes about great houses as epitomes of class and wealth, which nearby lesser houses and streets pretentiously seek to emulate.

On several occasions, Dickens mentions places like these, all of which survive today, as indicators of wealth, though he does not always describe the locations in detail. In *Dombey and Son*, the 'Honourable Mrs Skewton' had once 'borrowed a house in Brook Street, Grosvenor Square'. Tite Barnacle, in *Little Dorrit*, lives in Grosvenor Square, 'or very near it'. This is a mark of these characters' social pretensions as well as their probable wealth. In Dickens' writing, these place-names are markers of wealth, but the places are not described in detail, which creates the effect of knowing of them, but only from a distance, only as names of places outside his experience.

GROSVENOR SQUARE

In one of the early *Sketches by Boz*, Grosvenor Square, in Mayfair, is used in exactly this way as an arbitrary signifier of wealth in Boz's fantasy of a chimney sweep's restoration to his true noble status.

> We remember, in our young days, a little sweep about our own age, with curly hair and white teeth, whom we devoutly and sincerely believed to be the lost son and heir of some illustrious personage – an impression which was resolved into an unchangeable conviction on our infant mind, by the subject of our speculations informing us,

one day, in reply to our question, propounded a few moments before his ascent to the summit of the kitchen chimney, 'that he believed he'd been born in the vurkis, but he'd never know'd his father'. We felt certain from that time forth that he would one day be owned by a lord, at least; and we never heard the church-bells ring, or saw a flag hoisted in the neighbourhood, without thinking that the happy event had at last occurred, and that his long-lost parent had arrived in a coach and six, to take him home to Grosvenor-square. ('The First of May', *SB*)

Dickens was often attracted to the idea of a boy's restoration to rank. He developed this plotline more fully in *Oliver Twist*, where Oliver, like the chimney sweep, is born in a workhouse, but (unlike the sweep) goes on to learn of his true parentage and to be restored to his rightful status. Oliver finally comes to live in Mr Brownlow's comfortable middle-class abode in Clerkenwell, but until that point wealthy areas of London had been as unfamiliar to him as they so often are in Dickens' writing: Oliver is taken to lower-class Smithfield, 'although it might have been Grosvenor Square for anything Oliver knew to the contrary'. Dickens rehearsed the same stories of hidden riches and uncovered parentage throughout his writing career, in novels including *Nicholas Nickleby*, *Little Dorrit*, *Great Expectations* and others.

There were deeply personal reasons for Dickens' interest in the story of a boy discovering an unknown entitlement to wealth and gentility and being taken to live in the affluent parts of London. Throughout his lifetime he was haunted by the perceived indignity of being sent to work in a blacking factory as a boy, to the extent that he kept it a secret from all but his friend and biographer, John Forster, not even telling his own wife. He found the experience humiliating and beneath him and Oliver Twist's experience of remaining uncorrupted by the worst associates due to an innate goodness, is often seen to be a kind of self-description on Dickens' part.

Dickens wrote about his experience in his 'Autobiographical Fragment', brought to light by Forster only after his death.

But I held some station at the blacking warehouse too. Besides that my relative at the counting-house did what a man so occupied, and dealing with a thing so anomalous, could, to treat me as one upon a different footing from the rest. I never said, to man or boy, how it was that I came to be there, or gave the least indication of being sorry that I was there. That I suffered in secret, and that I suffered exquisitely, no one ever knew but I. How much I suffered, it is, as I have said already, utterly beyond my power to tell. No man's imagination can overstep the reality. But I kept my own counsel, and I did my work. I knew from the first, that if I could not do my work as well as any of the rest, I could not hold myself above slight and contempt. I soon became at least as expeditious and as skilful with my hands, as either of the other boys. Though perfectly familiar with them, my conduct and manners were different enough from theirs to place a space between us. They, and the men, always spoke of me as 'the young gentleman'. (*AF*)[1]

In *Oliver Twist* it is only ruffians and rogues, mostly Fagin's juvenile pickpockets, that are known, facetiously, as 'young gentlemen'. That is, until the novel's final chapter, where Oliver, finally restored to his true middle-class status, accompanies his guardian to Newgate Prison to see Fagin hanged. The turnkey asks Mr Brownlow, 'is the young gentleman to come too, sir?', unwittingly restoring the appropriate term of address to the boy. The chimney sweep in that early sketch never makes it to Grosvenor Square however, only to King's Cross, then called Battle Bridge. That Dickens is thinking of a possible version of his own life, in writing about the sweep, is hinted at by his aside that the sweep was then 'about our own age'. It is also evident in the application of his own remembered title to the boy:

[The unknown parent] never came, however; and, at the present moment, *the young gentleman* in question is settled down as a master sweep in the neighbourhood of Battle Bridge, his distinguishing characteristics being a decided antipathy to washing himself, and the possession of a pair of legs very inadequate to the support of his somewhat unwieldy and corpulent body. ('The First of May', *SB* [emphasis mine])

These personal details and affiliations suggest that one strand of Dickens' attitude to the affluent parts of London is his own boyhood sense of the injustice of his being excluded from them, as if against the rightful order.

MANSION HOUSE

In his 1853 essay, 'Gone Astray', Dickens returns to the idea of his young self looking in on London's richest properties, where he dreams of being welcomed and anticipates belonging, but finds himself violently shut out from them. In this case his aspirations are directed towards the Mansion House, the magnificent Georgian town palace in the City, which is still home to London's Lord Mayor:

> There was a dinner preparing at the Mansion House, and when I peeped in a grated kitchen window, and saw the men cooks at work in their white caps, my heart began to beat with hope that the Lord Mayor, or the Lady Mayoress, or one of the young Princesses their daughters, would look out of an upper apartment and direct me to be taken in. But, nothing of the kind occurred. It was not until

I had been peeping in some time that one of the cooks called to me (the window was open) 'Cut away, you sir!' which frightened me so, on account of his black whiskers, that I instantly obeyed. ('Gone Astray', *SJ*)

Although Dickens' young self imagines being 'taken in' by the mayoral family, by believing his own fictions about his ascent to riches he is only 'taken in' in that other sense, of being gulled, duped, deceived. The young Dickens remains on the outside.

GOLDEN SQUARE, SOHO

For all Dickens' social aspirations and his boyhood feeling that he somehow belonged in the wealthy quarters of London, he had little time for those who had only pretensions to wealth. He often housed these characters in areas of London that had been built for aristocracy but that were no longer occupied by the rich, though retaining faded traces of their former opulence. As London grew as a centre of industry and private commerce in the nine-teenth century, the burgeoning professional class increasingly took up residence in the areas being vacated by the dwindling upper classes. The large houses of the nobility, in Golden Square, Soho, for example, were divided up into smaller units, to be rented out to tenants and to London's large migrant population, with visitors often coming to London for short periods on business.

Dickens describes a house in a street just off Golden Square in *David Copperfield* (1849-50) when Martha takes David to London in search of Em'ly.

> We alighted at one of the entrances to the Square she had mentioned, where I directed the coach to wait, not knowing but that we might have some occasion for it. She laid her hand on my arm, and hurried me on to one of the sombre streets, of which there are several in that part, where the houses were once fair dwellings in the occupation of single families, but have, and had, long degenerated into poor lodgings let off in rooms. Entering at the open door of one of these, and releasing my arm, she beckoned me to follow her up the common staircase … It was a broad panelled staircase, with massive balustrades of some dark wood; cornices above the doors, ornamented with carved fruit and flowers; and broad seats in the windows. But all these tokens of past grandeur were miserably decayed and dirty; rot, damp, and age, had weakened the flooring, which in many places was unsound and even unsafe. Some attempts had been made, I noticed, to infuse new blood into this dwindling frame, by repairing the costly old wood-work here and there with common deal; but it was like the marriage of a reduced old noble to a plebeian pauper, and each party to the ill-assorted union shrunk away from the other. (*DC*, 50)

Ralph Nickleby lives in Golden Square and enjoys the cachet it brings him. He benefits from the prestige of having the address, though the nature of his business is indistinct.

> Although a few members of the graver professions live about Golden Square, it is not exactly in anybody's way to or from anywhere. It is one of the squares that have been; a quarter of the town that has gone down in the world, and taken to letting lodgings. Many of its first and second floors are let, furnished, to single gentlemen, and it takes boarders besides. It is a great resort of foreigners. The dark-complexioned men who wear large rings, and heavy watch-guards, and bushy whiskers, and who congregate under the Opera Colonnade, and about the box-office in the season, between four and five in the afternoon, when

They give away their orders,– all live in Golden Square, or within a street of it. Two or three violins and a wind instrument from the Opera band reside within its precincts. Its boarding-houses are musical, and the notes of pianos and harps float in the evening time round the head of the mournful statue, the guardian genius of a little wilderness of shrubs, in the centre of the square. On a summer's night, windows are thrown open, and groups of swarthy mustachioed men are seen by the passer-by, lounging at the casements, and smoking fearfully. Sounds of gruff voices practising vocal music invade the evening's silence, and the fumes of choice tobacco scent the air. There, snuff and cigars, and German pipes and flutes, and violins, and violoncellos, divide the supremacy between them. It is the region of song and smoke. Street bands are on their mettle in Golden Square, and itinerant glee-singers quaver involuntarily as they raise their voices within its boundaries.

This would not seem a spot very well adapted to the transaction of business; but Mr. Ralph Nickleby had lived there, notwithstanding, for many years, and uttered no complaint on that score. He knew nobody round about, and nobody knew him, although he enjoyed the reputation of being immensely rich. The tradesmen held that he was a sort of lawyer, and the other neighbours opined that he was a kind of general agent; both of which guesses were as correct and definite as guesses about other people's affairs usually are, or need to be. (*NN*, 2)

As a 'great resort of foreigners', characterised by varieties of musical expression, by this stage in the nineteenth century, Golden Square had become a parody of its former cosmopolitan culture. In the eighteenth century it had been home to numerous distinguished foreign artists and musicians. Now its itinerant population from Europe took up temporary lodgings in the hotels and boarding houses newly established in the square for their benefit, alongside the houses of professional men and later commercial firms.[2]

CADOGAN PLACE

If Ralph Nickleby benefits from the prestige of an address in Golden Square, though it did not quite sustain its former reputation, the same could be said of other of that novel's characters, the obnoxiously pretentious Mr and Mrs Wititterly, who live in Cadogan Place, off Sloane Street, in Belgravia. Dickens characterises it as awkwardly poised between two kinds of London life:

> Cadogan Place is the one slight bond that joins two great extremes; it is the connecting link between the aristocratic pavements of Belgrave Square and the barbarism of Chelsea. It is in Sloane Street, but not of it. The people in Cadogan Place look down upon Sloane Street, and think Brompton low. They affect fashion too, and wonder where the New Road is. Not that they claim to be on precisely the same footing as the high folks of Belgrave Square, and Grosvenor Place, but that they stand, with reference to them, rather in the light of those illegitimate children of the great who are content to boast of their connexions, although their connexions disavow them. Wearing as much as they can of the airs and semblances of loftiest rank, the people of Cadogan Place have the realities of middle station. It is the

conductor which communicates to the inhabitants of regions beyond its limit, the shock of pride of birth and rank, which it has not within itself, but derives from a fountain-head beyond; or, like the ligament which unites the Siamese twins, it contains something of the life and essence of two distinct bodies, and yet belongs to neither. (*NN*, 21)

OXFORD STREET AND MAYFAIR

Unlike Cadogan Place, Oxford Street and the area around it was secure of its position as one of the most salubrious areas in London. When Dickens writes about Oxford Street, he does so mindful of the large, imposing buildings that dominate it, and with some of that childhood sense of intimidation and exclusion from them. Oxford Street is re-envisioned in an experimental essay in *Sketches by Boz*, 'Early Coaches'. He asks the reader to imagine getting up at dawn to catch the first stage-coach of the day. The walk to the coach house at Charing Cross begins along Oxford Street:

A thaw, by all that is miserable! The frost is completely broken up. You look down the long perspective of Oxford-street, the gas-lights mournfully reflected on the wet pavement, and can discern no speck in the road to encourage the belief that there is a cab or a coach to be had – the very coachmen have gone home in despair. The cold sleet is drizzling down with that gentle regularity, which betokens a duration of four-and-twenty hours at least; the damp hangs upon the house-tops, and lamp-posts, and clings to you like an invisible cloak. The water is 'coming in' in every area, the pipes have burst, the water-butts are running over; the kennels seem to be doing matches against time, pump-handles descend of their own accord, horses in market-carts fall down, and there's no one to help them up again, policemen look as if they had been carefully sprinkled with powdered glass; here and there a milk-woman trudges slowly along, with a bit of list round each foot to keep her from slipping; boys who 'don't sleep in the house', and are not allowed much sleep out of it, can't wake their masters by thundering at the shop-door, and cry with cold – the compound of ice, snow, and water on the pavement, is a couple of inches thick – nobody ventures to walk fast to keep himself warm, and nobody could succeed in keeping himself warm if he did. ('Early Coaches', *SB*)

This is an eerie transformation of Oxford Street as Dickens would have known it, though he probably also saw it in the early hours. The familiar thoroughfare is disturbingly unfamiliar in this scene, as its 'long perspective' is witnessed from a new perspective. It is an impressionistic snapshot that captures an isolated moment in time – 'the water-butts are running over' – but that also seems to be a common occurrence. It creates an uncanny effect whereby the scene is both momentary and repeating, both specific and general. For example, 'here and there a milk-woman trudges slowly along, with a bit of list round each foot to keep her from slipping' – the detail of the cloth around the milk-woman's feet suggests the specific instance, but such a woman is seen 'here and there', as if she is a type. The hazy perspective prevents us from being sure what we are seeing, as if Dickens makes us feel what it is like to have risen up, half-asleep, to catch the first coach. When we are told of the boys who 'cry with cold' because they 'can't wake their masters by thundering at the shop-door', for example, we see before our mind's eye the boys' frantic hammering at the doors, but this may not be part of the scene that we are asked to envisage if it has already been given up as a lost cause or if it never took place because it was known in advance to be futile. This drama is eerily both there and not there.

As this book shows, the transformative capacity of Dickens' writing is frequently evident in his descriptions of London. Oxford Street is described again in *Little Dorrit* and although not so strikingly idiosyncratic a scenario as an early morning dash to catch the first coach, the cityscapes are again subject to a set of images, allusions, satirical thrusts, and personifications, as Dickens conveys a sense of the intimidating, melancholy, self-corroding atmosphere of the area, that is both one of his and his characters' impressions of the region.

Arthur Clennam and Mr Meagles arrive in Oxford Street in their search for Miss Wade and Tattycoram. They venture beyond it into the streets surrounding Park Lane and Grosvenor Square.

It was now summer-time; a grey, hot, dusty evening. They rode to the top of Oxford Street, and, there alighting, dived in among the great streets of melancholy stateliness, and the little streets that try to be as stately and succeed in being more melancholy, of which there is a labyrinth near Park Lane. Wildernesses of corner-houses, with barbarous old porticoes and appurtenances; horrors that came into existence under some wrong-headed person in some wrong-headed time, still demanding the blind admiration of all ensuing generations and determined to do so until they tumbled down; frowned upon the twilight. Parasite little tenements with the cramp in their whole frame, from the dwarf hall-door on the giant model of His Grace's in the Square, to the squeezed window of the boudoir commanding the dunghills in the Mews, made the evening doleful. Ricketty dwellings of undoubted fashion, but of a capacity to hold nothing comfortably except a dismal smell, looked like the last result of the great mansions' breeding in and in; and, where their little supplementary bows and balconies were supported on thin iron columns, seemed to be scrofulously resting upon crutches. Here and there a Hatchment, with the whole science of Heraldry in it, loomed down upon the street, like an Archbishop discoursing on Vanity. (*LD*, I, 27)

This account includes Dickens' familiar trick of describing the houses and streets that abut the most affluent areas as if somehow trying to emulate them, and in suggesting that these lesser houses are like the 'last result of the great mansions' breeding-in-and-in', he takes a swipe at the aristocracy that traditionally inhabited the area. This passage expertly conveys a sense of walking through these imposing streets faced down by the blank aspect of the intimidating buildings, as Clennam and Little Dorrit are, in their forlorn search for Miss Wade and Tattycoram. It does so especially in those sentences ending in 'frowned upon the twilight' and 'made the evening doleful', which delay their verbs, while noun builds upon noun, and clause digresses after clause. They convey the way you can walk up and down the surroundings of Oxford Street, seeing building upon building, and road upon road, but with little relating to the matter at hand that would move events forward.

Oxford Street, now well known as the home of major chains' flagship stores, was becoming a centre for shops in the 1850s when Dickens wrote *Little Dorrit*. He depicts, with wry wit, the aloofness of the shopping establishments in the area at this time:

The shops, few in number, made no show; for popular opinion was as nothing to them. The pastry-cook knew who was on his books, and in that knowledge could be calm, with a few glass cylinders of dowager peppermint-drops in his window, and half-a-dozen ancient specimens of currant jelly. A few oranges formed the greengrocer's whole concession to the vulgar mind. A single basket made of moss, once containing plovers' eggs, held all that the poulterer had to say to the rabble. (*LD*, I, 27)

HARLEY STREET AND CAVENDISH SQUARE

In his description of Harley Street, also in *Little Dorrit*, where it is the home of the ill-fated banker, Mr Merdle, Dickens responds again to the imposing blankness of the great houses. He develops a comic suggestion that it reflects the similarly

dumb blankness of their inhabitants, whom he imagines arranged against each other across a dinner table, much in the manner of the houses in the street, so that the rows of houses that are 'opposing' one another seem not just to be facing each other but to be somehow adversarial.

[T]he opposing rows of houses in Harley Street were very grim with one another. Indeed, the mansions and their inhabitants were so much alike in that respect, that the people were often to be found drawn up on opposite sides of dinner-tables, in the shade of their own loftiness, staring at the other side of the way with the dullness of the houses.

Everybody knows how like the street, the two dinner-rows of people who take their stand by the street will be. The expressionless uniform twenty houses, all to be knocked at and rung at in the same form, all approachable by the same dull steps, all fended off by the same pattern of railing, all with the same impracticable fire-escapes, the same inconvenient fixtures in their heads, and everything without exception to be taken at a high valuation – who has not dined with these? The house so drearily out of repair, the occasional bow-window, the stuccoed house, the newly-fronted house, the corner house with nothing but angular rooms, the house with the blinds always down, the house with the hatchment always up, the house where the collector has called for one quarter of an Idea, and found nobody at home – who has not dined with these? The house that nobody will take, and is to be had a bargain – who does not

know her? The showy house that was taken for life by the
disappointed gentleman, and which doesn't suit him at all – who is
unacquainted with that haunted habitation? (*LD*, II, 21)

In 1858 Harley Street had not yet acquired its reputation for
being a home of medical practitioners, though this was only a
few years away. It was known to be a haven of the rich, which is
why the Merdles are able and content to live there. It was exactly
the kind of street that Dickens as a boy found intimidating and
beyond his experience, if not his aspirations. While a sense of
distaste and apprehension remains in his description of Harley
Street and Cavendish Square, it is a mark of Dickens' immense
financial and popular success as a novelist by this stage in his
career that he is now able to appeal to common knowledge
of the dining habits of the wealthy who move about in high
society – 'who has not dined with these?' What's more, at the
height of his fame, Dickens did in fact receive invitations to
dine at the Mansion House. In the end, affluent London was
not so unfamiliar to Dickens after all.

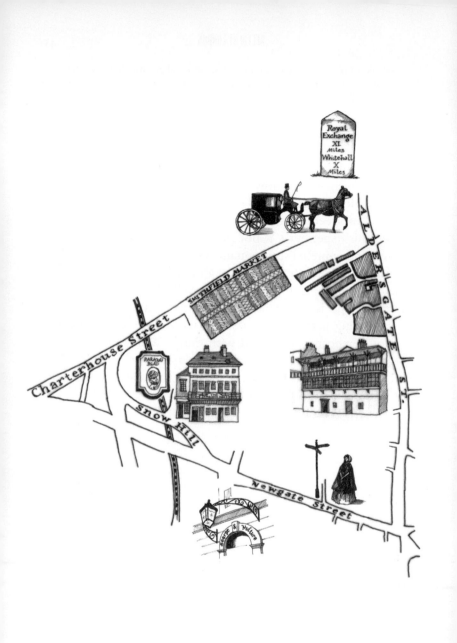

COACH HOUSES & HOTELS

The beginning of Dickens' writing career coincided very closely with the advent of the horse-drawn omnibus carriage and the demise of the hackney cab, as well as the older hackney coaches. Hackney coaches were of long standing. These were the stage coaches, prominent since the sixteenth century, by which Britons travelled across the country, moving from city to city. In the nineteenth century, short-stages were introduced, in addition, to run within large cities, although they were never well suited to urban work. Hackney cabriolets were of more recent origin. These were horse-drawn, two-wheeled vehicles with one driver and room for two passengers inside. Hackney cabs were popular throughout the twenties and thirties, but were soon rivalled by omnibuses. Omnibuses were horse-drawn, long, boxy vehicles that could carry between twelve and twenty-two passengers, depending on design. They initially worked the route between Paddington and the Bank, although other routes were soon added and the cost of travel gradually declined throughout the century.[1] There are four *Sketches by Boz* devoted to the vagaries of London's public transport: 'Omnibuses' (1834); 'Hackney Coach Stands' (1835); 'Early Coaches' (1835); and 'The Last Cab Driver and the First Omnibus Cad' (1836). In them, Dickens takes a comic look at these archetypal forms of London transport, and he does so with special relish, knowing that the hackney coach and the hackney cab are both on their way out of common use.

These pieces draw several parallels between means of being transported around London and that other way we can move from place to place in the city: by reading a narrative about it. The parallels are developed in Dickens' first full-length novel, *The Pickwick Papers*, where the plot is extended from one coach journey to another. Coach houses and taverns are therefore staging posts during the progress of Dickens' plots and they are returned to again and again, both as latent springs of further action and as reminders of what has been accomplished since the last arrival at the same point.

For the Pickwickians, as for many Londoners, the terminus of these journeys usually featured a tavern or a hotel. These were an important part of London's transport network – not least because they were part of a national network, as well as a metropolitan one. The hotels benefited from the fact that they were points of arrival for visitors coming to London, as well as a place of departure and provision for those leaving. Coaching inns were clustered on the main roads out of London, such as Piccadilly, Oxford Street, Bishopsgate, Aldgate and Borough High Street. They included the Bull and Mouth, Aldersgate, the George and Blue Boar, Holborn, Cross Keys in Gracechurch Street, the Nag's Head in the Borough, and the Saracen's Head, Snow Hill. [2]

Covent Garden was also an important coaching yard. In the sketch 'Early Coaches', the imagined traveller heads here first thing in the morning to catch the coach to Birmingham:

> You arrive at the office, and look wistfully up the yard for the Birmingham High-flier, which, for aught you can see, may have flown away altogether, for no preparations appear to be on foot for the departure of any vehicle in the shape of a coach. ('Early Coaches', *SB*)

This sketch about the exasperating miseries of travelling first thing in the morning is written in a hypothetical second-person, as if to say, 'isn't it always the way?' Here, Dickens pokes fun at the absurd promotional hypocrisy of a coach called the 'High-flier' that does not even turn up on time, by suspecting it to have 'flown away altogether'. The joke is continued by the use of the idiom 'on foot' to mean 'underway', which indirectly hints at the comic possibility that the traveller will be forced to walk to Birmingham if the coach fails to show.

Dickens wrote with playful over-enthusiasm about coach travel, as opposed to the newer (but still dated) mode of transport in hackney cabs. The last paragraph of his sketch, 'Hackney

Coach Stands', enjoys the shabby gentility of the coaches, which he imagines as holding on to their former glory:

> A hackney-cab has always been a hackney-cab, from his first entry into public life; whereas a hackney-coach is a remnant of past gentility, a victim to fashion, a hanger-on of an old English family, wearing their arms, and, in days of yore, escorted by men wearing their livery, stripped of his finery, and thrown upon the world, like a once-smart footman when he is no longer sufficiently juvenile for his office, progressing lower and lower in the scale of four-wheeled degradation, until at last it comes to – *a stand!* ('Hackney Coach Stands', *SB*)

There is a light pun on the general, figurative sense of coming to a stand (a standstill) and its more specific reference in the context of coach travel (a coach stand), but the emphatic italics of '*a stand!*' primarily draw attention to the way that the sentence itself grinds to a halt, like a hackney coach. The parallel is reinforced because this is the last sentence in the sketch, so the whole essay comes to rest at the word 'stand'. The last paragraph of 'Early Coaches' recognises a similar parallel. It ends with the coach travellers 'looking forward as anxiously to the termination of our journey, as we fear our readers will have done, long since, to the conclusion of our paper'. Dickens' suggestion that the anxious expectations of the travellers match those of his forbearing readers provides part of the self-deprecating humour by which the young writer forged friendly relations with his increasingly admiring public.

Since Dickens often brings his sketches to a conclusion by linking his own narrative to the main theme of the paper, together, the sketches relating to London's transport systems provide a set of investigations into the symmetries between coach travel and narrative. These symmetries would inform many of his novels, from *The Pickwick Papers* on, where coaching inns and hotels feature at important stages in the characters' travels and in their lives.

THE GEORGE AND VULTURE

In Dickens' first novel, the miscellaneous adventures of Mr Pickwick and his companions take place in London and variously across the south of England and the Midlands. The Pickwickians travel about, usually in hackney coaches, occasionally in cabs, and are seasoned inhabitants of coach houses and hotels. Their most frequent watering hole is the 'George and Vulture Tavern and Hotel, George Yard, Lombard Street', near the Bank of England and in the historic centre of the City of London. The George and Vulture still stands today.

The tavern was frequented by Dickens on occasions so he would have known it well. Like most taverns, it had a bar room downstairs, where there were also public lounges, and rooms for rent upstairs. Being a public house, the George and Vulture is the scene of many meetings and transactions in the novel, in a way that a private home would not be. That is why Mr Pickwick is able to invite people to join him for dinner there, which he does, promiscuously at the Browdies' wedding:

> Long before Mr. Pickwick was weary of dancing, the newly-married couple had retired from the scene. There was a glorious supper down stairs, notwithstanding, and a good long sitting after it; and when Mr. Pickwick awoke, late the next morning, he had a confused recollection of having, severally and confidentially, invited somewhere about five-and-forty people to dine with him at the George and Vulture, the very first time they came to London; which Mr. Pickwick rightly considered a pretty certain indication of his having taken something besides exercise, on the previous night. (*PP*, 28)

The temporary home of itinerant inhabitants, the George and Vulture is not only the setting for some of the novel's scenes, but also a point of departure from where the Pickwickians set out on their next adventure.

THE SARACEN'S HEAD

In *Nicholas Nickleby* (1838), it is the Saracen's Head in Snow Hill that is the departure point for Nicholas's adventures in the north of England and it is here that he first meets Squeers. Squeers advertises for an assistant at his Yorkshire school and chooses the tavern as a suitable rendezvous: 'Mr Squeers is in town, and attends daily, from one till four, at the Saracen's Head, Snow Hill.' The Saracen's Head is the obvious choice for Squeers because, coming down from Yorkshire, he could have arrived at the coach yard overlooked by the inn, which was accustomed to provide temporary lodgings for travellers. The Saracen's Head, which survived until 1868, when it was demolished, serviced routes to most parts of the country: its best known coaches going to Birmingham and to Leeds. While the Saracen's Head was for this reason an accurate choice for Dickens, the name itself was expressive of Squeers' status in London as a fierce outsider. It anticipates his barbarism even before it is known to the reader or to Nicholas. Dickens lets his imagination run free on the associations conjured up by the name of the tavern and by 'Snow Hill', names loosed from the reality of their signified locations by their presence on the back of the stage coaches:

Snow Hill! What kind of place can the quiet town's-people who see the words emblazoned, in all the legibility of gilt letters and dark shading, on the north-country coaches, take Snow Hill to be? All people have some undefined and shadowy notion of a place whose name is frequently before their eyes, or often in their ears. What a vast number of random ideas there must be perpetually floating about, regarding this same Snow Hill. The name is such a good one. Snow Hill – Snow Hill too, coupled with a Saracen's Head: picturing to us by a double association of ideas, something stern and rugged! A bleak desolate tract of country, open to piercing blasts and fierce wintry storms – a dark, cold, and gloomy heath, lonely by day, and scarcely to be thought of by honest folks at night – a place which solitary wayfarers shun, and where desperate robbers congregate;– this, or something like this, should be the prevalent notion of Snow Hill in those remote and rustic parts, through which the Saracen's Head, like some grim apparition, rushes each day and night with mysterious and ghost-like punctuality; holding its swift and headlong course in all weathers, and seeming to bid defiance to the very elements themselves. (*NN*, 4)

Dickens notes that the reality is rather different, and remarks on the proximity of Snow Hill to Newgate Prison. Then he continues:

Near to the jail, and by consequence near to Smithfield also, and the Compter and the bustle and noise of the city; and just on that particular part of Snow Hill where omnibus horses going eastward seriously think of falling down on purpose, and where horses in hackney cabriolets going westward not unfrequently fall by accident, is the coachyard of the Saracen's-Head Inn: its portal guarded by two Saracens' heads and shoulders, which it was once the pride and glory of the choice spirits of this metropolis to pull down at night, but which have for some time remained in undisturbed tranquillity; possibly because this species of humour is now confined to Saint James's parish, where door knockers are preferred, as being more portable, and bell-wires esteemed as convenient tooth-picks. Whether this be the reason or not, there they are, frowning upon you from each side of the gateway, and the inn itself, garnished with another Saracen's Head, frowns upon you from the top of the yard; while from the door of the hind boot of all the red coaches that are standing therein, there glares a small Saracen's Head, with a twin expression to the large Saracens' Heads below, so that the general appearance of the pile is of the Saracenic order.

When you walk up this yard, you will see the booking-office on your left, and the tower of St Sepulchre's church darting abruptly up into the sky on your right, and a gallery of bed-rooms on both sides. Just before you, you will observe a long window with the words 'coffee-room' legibly painted above it; and looking out of that window, you would have seen in addition, if you had gone at the right time, Mr. Wackford Squeers with his hands in his pockets.

Mr. Squeers's appearance was not prepossessing. He had but one eye, and the popular prejudice runs in favour of two. The eye he had was unquestionably useful, but decidedly not ornamental; being of a greenish grey, and in shape resembling the fan-light of a street door. (*NN*, 4)

The lively description of the scene is as playful as it is ominous, but there is one moment when Dickens' traumatic boyhood experience is imprinted on the account. During his miserable time at the blacking warehouse, the young Dickens would often take himself to local coffee houses during his half an hour teatime break. He recalls these occasions in his 'Autobiographical Fragment':

> The coffee-shops to which I most resorted were, one in Maiden-lane; one in a court (non-existent now) close to Hungerford-market; and one in St. Martin's-lane, of which I only recollect that it stood near the church, and that in the door there was an oval glass-plate, with coffee-room painted on it, addressed towards the street. If I ever find myself in a very different kind of coffee-room now, but where there is such an inscription on glass, and read it backward on the wrong side MOOR-EEFFOC (as I often used to do then, in a dismal reverie), a shock goes through my blood. (*AF*)

Coffee rooms appear frequently in Dickens' fiction. Often they are associated with the sort of awkwardness and discomfort that had been his own experience in them as a boy. On this occasion in *Nicholas Nickleby*, the particular attention that is directed to the words 'coffee-room' above the window suggest the painful recollection of his own childhood on Dickens' part, whether consciously or not.

After a successful interview with Squeers, Nicholas goes back to the Saracen's Head to meet his new employer for the return journey to Yorkshire. On this second visit, Nicholas witnesses Squeers giving his boys watered-down milk for breakfast, which presages the cruelty the novel's hero will experience in the coming chapters.

The Saracen's Head is subsequently the station for journeys to and from Yorkshire. When John Browdie takes his new wife, Tilda, to London for their honeymoon, it is to the Saracen's Head that they go – although, appropriately for a man whose heart is softened by love, he mistakenly thinks its name is the more gentle 'Sarah Son's Head'. The play on the name may, in fact, be a private joke on Dickens' part, for the benefit of those of his contemporaries familiar with the inn, because the Saracen's Head was at that time run by a woman named Sarah – Sarah Mountain, although she was succeeded in the business by her son, who claimed that he had been running the place since 1821.[3] They find themselves 'startled by the noise of loud and angry threatening below-stairs, which presently attained so high a pitch, and were conveyed besides in language so towering, sanguinary and ferocious, that it could hardly have been surpassed, if there had actually been a Saracen's head then present in the establishment, supported on the shoulders and surmounting the trunk of a real, live, furious, and most unappeasable Saracen' (*NN*, 43). Once the brawl has quietened, they are surprised to meet Frank Cheeryble. The chapter in which these meetings take place Dickens describes as officiating 'as a kind of gentleman usher, in bringing various people together', which is a function not only of chapters but of London's coach houses in Dickens' work.

The tavern again features when Squeers returns to London later in the novel, and once again when Nicholas is persuaded to make another trip to Yorkshire, accompanied by his sister, Kate, to visit the Browdies: 'Thus it was that between seven and eight o'clock one evening, he and Kate found themselves in the Saracen's Head booking-office, securing a place to Greta Bridge by the next morning's coach' (*NN*, 64). That evening his conversation with Kate proceeds apace as 'the place they had just been in called up so many recollections'. Thus coach houses in Dickens acquire associations through the course of the narrative, by being connected to some of the most eventful episodes in the plot.

THE GOLDEN CROSS

In *David Copperfield*, the Golden Cross, a hotel at Charing Cross, becomes indelibly associated with momentous events in David's life. Charing Cross was a major terminus on the metropolitan and national coach routes, with frequent departures to Dover, Brighton, Bristol and York. A hotel called the Golden Cross had long been established there, but it has since been demolished. In the novel, the Golden Cross reminds David of Steerforth and, consequently, of Steerforth's devastating elopement with Little Em'ly. One reason for these associations held by the hotel is the deep way in which David's perception of it was transformed by Steerforth. David's first experience of the hotel was somewhat dismal and humbling:

> We went to the Golden Cross at Charing Cross, then a mouldy sort of establishment in a close neighbourhood. A waiter showed me

into the coffee-room; and a chambermaid introduced me to my small bedchamber, which smelt like a hackney-coach, and was shut up like a family vault. I was still painfully conscious of my youth, for nobody stood in any awe of me at all: the chambermaid being utterly indifferent to my opinions on any subject, and the waiter being familiar with me, and offering advice to my inexperience.

'Well now,' said the waiter, in a tone of confidence, 'what would you like for dinner? Young gentlemen likes poultry in general, have a fowl!'

I told him, as majestically as I could, that I wasn't in the humour for a fowl. (*DC*, 19)

With Dickens' time in the blacking factory in mind, we should not be surprised that the site of David's feelings of humiliation is a coffee-room. His discomfort has not changed the next day, immediately before meeting Steerforth:

When the chambermaid tapped at my door at eight o'clock, and informed me that my shaving-water was outside, I felt severely the having no occasion for it, and blushed in my bed. The suspicion that she laughed too, when she said it, preyed upon my mind all the time I was dressing; and gave me, I was conscious, a sneaking and guilty air when I passed her on the staircase, as I was going down to breakfast. I was so sensitively aware, indeed, of being younger than I could have wished, that for some time I could not make up my mind to pass her at all, under the ignoble circumstances of the case; but, hearing her there with a broom, stood peeping out of window at King Charles on horse-back, surrounded by a maze of hackney-coaches and looking anything but regal in a drizzling rain and a dark-brown fog, until I was admonished by the waiter that the gentleman was waiting for me. (*DC*, 20)

David's impression of the statue of King Charles I on horseback is as coloured by his own mood as is his experience of the hotel. The statue of King Charles I, which remains at Charing Cross today, dates back to 1633 though it was erected in its present position only after the Restoration of Charles II. That King Charles looks 'anything but regal' reflects the downturn in David's own self-esteem. It is of a piece, for example, with his recent attempt to respond to the familiar waiter 'as majestically as I could'. But once in Steerforth's company, significantly 'not in the coffee-room', the hotel seems much more comfortable and welcoming:

It was not in the coffee-room that I found Steerforth expecting me, but in a snug private apartment, red-curtained and Turkey-carpeted, where the fire burnt bright, and a fine hot breakfast was set forth on a table covered with a clean cloth; and a cheerful miniature of the room, the fire, the breakfast, Steerforth, and all, was shining in the little round mirror over the sideboard. I was rather bashful at first, Steerforth being so selfpossessed, and elegant, and superior to me in all respects (age included); but his easy patronage soon put that to rights, and made me quite at home. I could not enough admire the change he had wrought in the Golden Cross; or compare the dull forlorn state I had held yesterday, with this morning's comfort and this morning's entertainment. As to the waiter's familiarity, it was quenched as if it had never been. He attended on us, as I may say, in sackcloth and ashes. (*DC*, 20)

It is Steerforth's blazing confidence as much as the fire that seems to light and heat the apartment. The effect of his seductive presence is relayed through the apparent warmth and elegance of the room, rather than directly. Indeed, David sees him in the mirror along with the fire and the breakfast. Steerforth's presence is so imprinted upon David's experience of the Golden Cross that even the 'fine hot breakfast' seems somehow suggestive of his friend, especially when Dickens chooses to write that it was 'set forth', a lexical choice that echoes Steerforth's name.

The indelible association of the Golden Cross inn with Steerforth reminds David later in the novel of the miserable consequences of Steerforth's actions. When he later meets Mr Peggotty he takes him to one of the public rooms there, at 'the inn so memorable to me in connexion with his misfortune'. When David later alights at the Gray's Inn Coffeehouse, it reminds him of that other of London's taverns: 'It recalled, at first, that so-different time when I had put up at the Golden Cross, and reminded me of the changes that had come to pass since then' (*DC*, 59). The Golden Cross is, as it were, a staging post in David's experiences, a constant that reminds him of how much else has changed, especially in connection with the events related to Steerforth, which are forever associated for him with the Golden Cross.

COVENT GARDEN LODGINGS

Like Charing Cross, Covent Garden was the terminus for several coach routes. When, in *Great Expectations* (1860-1), Pip jumps into a hackney coach on Fleet Street, after being warned 'Don't Go Home', by a mysterious message (from Wemmick as it later turns out), Covent Garden is his destination. He stays at the elegant Hummums Hotel. The Hummums was a famous hotel, located in the south-west corner of the Little Piazza at Covent Garden since the late seventeenth century.[4] It had originally housed Turkish baths and its unusual name echoes the Arabic word for baths, hammam. After several different incarnations, the hotel was demolished in 1885:

Turning from the Temple gate as soon as I had read the warning, I made the best of my way to Fleet-street, and there got a late hackney chariot and drove to the Hummums in Covent Garden. In those times a bed was always to be got there at any hour of the night, and the chamberlain, letting me in at his ready wicket, lighted the candle next in order on his shelf, and showed me straight into the bedroom next in order on his list. It was a sort of vault on the ground floor at the back, with a despotic monster of a four-post bedstead in it, straddling over the whole place, putting one of his arbitrary legs into the fireplace and another into the doorway, and squeezing the wretched little washing-stand in quite a Divinely Righteous manner. (*GE*, III, 6)

They are telling details that the chamberlain 'lighted the candle next in order on his shelf' and that Pip is taken to the 'bedroom next in order on his list'. For as much as hotels aspire to homeliness, Pip knows his room to be simply one of many, all alike, and available at a set price. The indifference of his welcome is such that he might wonder if in being put up at the hotel, he is merely being put up with. It is an irony that while hotels purport to offer a home from home, at the Hummums Pip is made dizzyingly aware, as he passes a restless night, that this is a place to retreat to when he needs not to go home:

What a doleful night! How anxious, how dismal, how long! There was an inhospitable smell in the room, of cold soot and hot dust; and, as I looked up into the corners of the tester over my head, I thought what a number of bluebottle flies from the butchers', and earwigs from the market, and grubs from the country, must be holding on up there, lying by for next summer. This led me to speculate whether any of them ever tumbled down, and then I fancied that I felt light falls on my face – a disagreeable turn of thought, suggesting other and more objectionable approaches up my back. When I had lain awake a little while, those extraordinary voices with which silence teems, began to make themselves audible. The closet whispered, the fireplace sighed, the little washing-stand ticked, and one guitarstring played occasionally in the chest of drawers. At about the same time, the eyes on the wall acquired a new expression, and in every one of those staring rounds I saw written, Don't go home. (*GE*, III, 6)

This episode is a maniacally heightened example of that characteristic of Dickens' writing about hotels and coaching houses where the rooms are sufficiently uniform and nondescript to be experienced idiosyncratically according to the subjective perspectives of the traveller.

In *Little Dorrit*, it is Arthur Clennam's unnamed lodgings in Covent Garden that are described when the novel first defiantly turns its attention to Little Dorrit's point of view. Arthur Clennam is indifferent to his 'dim room', but Amy Dorrit, when she arrives, sees it differently:

> Arthur Clennam rose hastily, and saw her standing at the door. This history must sometimes see with Little Dorrit's eyes, and shall begin that course by seeing him.
>
> Little Dorrit looked into a dim room, which seemed a spacious one to her, and grandly furnished. Courtly ideas of Covent Garden, as a place with famous coffee-houses, where gentlemen wearing gold-laced coats and sword had quarrelled and fought duels; costly ideas of Covent Garden, as a place where there were flowers in winter at guineas a-piece, pine-apples at guineas a pound, and peas at guineas a pint; picturesque ideas of Covent Garden, as a place where there was a mighty theatre, showing wonderful and beautiful sights to richly-dressed ladies and gentlemen, and which was for ever far beyond the reach of poor Fanny or poor uncle; desolate ideas of Covent Garden, as having all those arches in it, where the miserable children in rags among whom she had just now passed, like young rats, slunk and hid, fed on offal, huddled together for warmth, and were hunted about (look to the rats young and old, all ye Barnacles, for before God they are eating away our foundations, and will bring the roofs on our heads!); teeming ideas of Covent Garden, as a place of past and present mystery, romance, abundance, want, beauty, ugliness, fair country gardens, and foul street-gutters, all confused together,– made the room dimmer than it was, in Little Dorrit's eyes, as they timidly saw it from the door.
>
> At first in the chair before the gone-out fire, and then turned round wondering to see her, was the gentleman whom she sought. (*LD*, I, 14)

It is a remarkable breadth of vision, a subjective panorama, and from it we learn as much about Amy Dorrit as we do about Covent Garden. Dickens' own voice intrudes too with the prophetic warning about the rat-like children. The evening meeting is unremarkable in many ways, but for Arthur and Amy, it makes an epoch in their shared history. When the Dorrits are released from the Marshalsea in the second book of the novel, Amy writes to Clennam from Venice and remembers the scene:

> do you remember one night when I came with Maggy to your lodging in Covent Garden? That room I have often and often fancied I have seen before me, travelling along for miles by the side of our carriage, when I have looked out of the carriage window after dark. We were shut out that night, and sat at the iron gate, and walked about till morning. (*LD*, II, 4)

As so often in Dickens' fiction, lodgings in coach yards become figurative as well as literal staging posts. The hotels and taverns remind characters of previous times when they passed through. The rooms themselves are charged with memories of earlier adventures and encounters. Amy Dorrit's appearance at Clennam's lodgings in Covent Garden becomes a memory for Arthur too. He is reminded of it when he watches Miss Wade and the orphan Tattycoram (named after the Coram orphanage) as they walk past Covent Garden:

> They crossed the Strand, and passed through Covent Garden (under the windows of his old lodging where dear Little Dorrit had come that night), and slanted away north-east, until they passed the great building whence Tattycoram derived her name, and turned into the Gray's Inn Road. (*LD*, II, 9)

Dickens delineates the tender feelings Arthur Clennam and Amy Dorrit have for each other with great tact and care in the novel, and this moment where Clennam watches two women who have no direct bearing on those emotions presents a fine example. The parenthetical observation that the lodging they pass is one that has its own private history for Clennam and Little Dorrit is unobtrusive but revealing, while the reference to 'dear Little Dorrit', at once that of the narrative voice and of Clennam himself, with the narrative focalised through his perspective, shows his fondness for his young friend. It is one of the most touching examples of the way that Dickens' London, and especially its coach houses and hotels, become imprinted with the experiences of his characters.

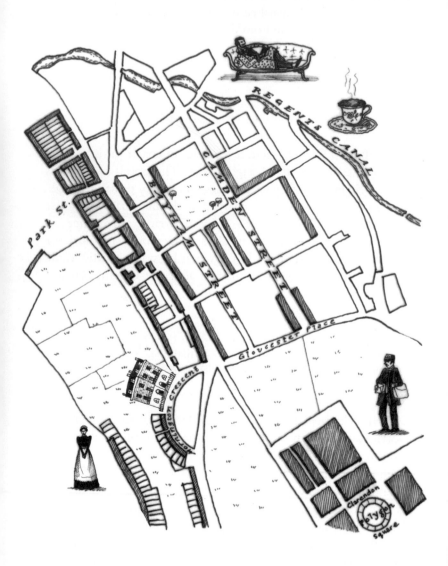

AT HOME IN LONDON

In much of Dickens' writing about areas of London he adopts the perspective of an outsider. Whether in the affluent areas or the urban slums, we envisage Dickens looking on from the fringes. He and his characters frequent coach houses and taverns, but often they do so because they are visitors, in the process of moving on. But London was, for most of his life, Dickens' home. Although the Dickens family spent a couple of years in the capital when Charles was three or four, they did not settle there until 1823 when he was eleven. Then they took up residence in Bayham Street in Camden Town, soon moving to Gower Street North in Somers Town, where Mrs Dickens hoped to set up a school to alleviate their financial worries. It didn't work. When his father was jailed for debt, the young Dickens took up lodgings in various parts of the city, whilst working at Warren's Blacking Factory. He continued to live in different places until he was married. Then he had more settled periods at Devonshire Terrace, near Regent's Park, and Tavistock House in Tavistock Square. Dickens left London in 1860, ten years before his death. During his last decade he continued to come to the capital to edit his journal, *All the Year Round*, whose offices were in Wellington Street, near Covent Garden, where Dickens would stay during his visits.

Although John Forster said about Dickens that, 'any special regard for houses he had lived in, was not a thing noticeable in him',[1] the appearance of some of these former homes in Dickens' fiction suggests that they carried more profound associations than Forster thought likely.[2] The houses that are most fully recreated in his novels are typically those in which his own experiences were formative. More often than not, these are the homes of his childhood in London, especially around the time when the Dickens family were sliding into debt; his lodgings when he worked in the blacking factory, and the accommodation he had when he courted and married Catherine Hogarth. Areas around Camden Town and Somers Town, where Dickens lived as a boy and again as a young adult, appear in his writing and contain the homes of Polly Toodles in *Dombey and Son*, one of Tommy Traddles' lodging places in *David Copperfield*, and Harold Skimpole's abode in *Bleak House*. David's stay in Lant Street was based on Dickens' time there and John Westlock (*Martin Chuzzlewit*) and Rosa Bud (*Edwin Drood*) both resided for a time in Furnival's Inn, where Dickens lived at the start of his writing career. Several critics and editors have noted the occasions when his characters' homes are inspired by the places where he had himself lived, observing similarities of detail or circumstances. Dickens' houses did not only provide the architectural originals for the homes of some of his characters. This chapter shows that, in the case of those houses that accommodated Dickens at formative periods of his life, his writing about his former homes is deeply invested with an alert sense of his own feelings and experiences of living there.

BAYHAM STREET, CAMDEN TOWN

When the Dickens family moved to London from Chatham in 1823, their first home was 16 Bayham Street in Camden Town, a small terrace in a blandly uniform row of houses. Camden Town was a largely residential area that had been built amid green fields in the late eighteenth century. The housing was uninspiring, so it was no great loss when the railway cut through the area in the 1840s. Bayham Street was one of the poorest areas of the city. Its tenements were demolished at the start of the twentieth century. Bayham Street itself is never mentioned by name in Dickens' novels but Camden Town and the surrounding area feature in several of his works – including, almost certainly, under the guise of 'Camberling Town' in *Dombey and Son*, home of Staggs's Gardens.

The time at Camden Town was not a happy one for the eleven year old Dickens. It was during the time at Bayham Street that his father's finances worsened and it became increasingly difficult to pay off his creditors. There was also a sadness at the removal from Chatham. In the 'Autobiographical Fragment', Dickens remembered his dejection: 'I thought in the little back garret of Bayham Street of all that I had lost in losing Chatham.' He would find some diversion in walking the streets, although his first experiences of the huge city must have been intimidating. From Bayham Street, he paid regular visits to his godfather's in Limehouse and to an uncle in Soho. He later returned to Camden Town when his father was in the debtors' prison and then he would walk each day to the blacking factory at Hungerford Stairs, near the Strand.

One of the earliest occurrences of Camden Town in Dickens' work is in *Oliver Twist*, and it is possible that his boyhood experience of walking the neighbouring streets plays a part in his description. Fagin tells one of his pickpockets, Noah Claypole, that Camden Town is a 'kinchin lay':

'What's that?' demanded Mr Claypole.

'The kinchins, my dear,' said the Jew, 'is the young children that's sent on errands by their mothers, with sixpences and shillings, and the lay is just to take their money away – they've always got it ready in their hands, – and then knock 'em into the kennel, and walk off very slow, as if there was nothing else the matter but a child fallen down and hurt itself. Ha! ha! ha!'

'Ha! ha!' roared Mr Claypole, kicking up his legs in an ecstasy. 'Lord, that's the very thing!'

'To be sure it is,' replied Fagin; 'and you can have a few good beats chalked out in Camden-Town, and Battle-Bridge, and neighbourhoods like that, where they're always going errands, and upset as many kinchins as you want, any hour in the day. Ha! ha! ha!' With this, Fagin poked Mr Claypole in the side, and they joined in a burst of laughter both long and loud. (*OT*, 42)

Fagin's choice of words mirrors his own ability to be both jocular and menacing: 'a few good beats' is a route for walking but it also suggests a pummelling; to 'upset' the kinchins is to make them cry, but also, more physically, to knock them over.

Haunts of pickpockets they may have been, but areas like Camden Town are more frequently thought of by Dickens as home to large numbers of legal clerks, who had moved to areas like these, on the periphery of central London. Accommodation was more affordable there than in London's legal heartlands, and so an increasing number of clerks and other professionals moved there with their families. In *Sketches by Boz*, Dickens describes this area of London first thing in the morning, when 'the early clerk population of Somers and Camden towns, Islington, and Pentonville, are fast pouring into the city; or directing their steps towards Chancery-lane and the Inns of Court', a migration he would have seen first hand when he lived at Bayham Street.

In *David Copperfield*, David goes to visit Traddles at his lodgings in Camden Town. Not knowing his way exactly he is pointed in the right direction by 'one of our clerks' who, not surprisingly, 'lived in that direction':

> I found that the street was not as desirable a one as I could have wished it to be, for the sake of Traddles. The inhabitants appeared to have a propensity to throw any little trifles they were not in want of, into the road: which not only made it rank and sloppy, but untidy too, on account of the cabbage-leaves. The refuse was not wholly vegetable either, for I myself saw a shoe, a doubled-up saucepan, a black bonnet, and an umbrella, in various stages of decomposition, as I was looking out for the number I wanted.
>
> The general air of the place reminded me forcibly of the days when I lived with Mr and Mrs Micawber. An indescribable character of faded gentility that attached to the house I sought, and made it unlike all the other houses in the street – though they were all built on one monotonous pattern, and looked like the early copies of a blundering boy who was learning to make houses, and had not yet got out of his cramped brick and mortar pothooks – reminded me still more of Mr and Mrs Micawber. Happening to arrive at the door as it was opened to the afternoon milkman, I was reminded of Mr and Mrs Micawber more forcibly yet.
>
> 'Now,' said the milkman to a very youthful servant-girl. 'Had that there little bill of mine been heerd on?' (*DC*, 27)

It turns out that Traddles is lodging at the Micawbers' new home and they are still struggling to pay their bills. That Mr and Mrs

Micawber should have been brought to mind as David approaches the house, however, is odd. It prepares the ground for David's subsequent discovery in the chapter that they do indeed now live there, but more than this, it is as if the lives of David and Dickens have become so entangled that Dickens' own memories are 'forcibly' pressing themselves upon his fictional hero. David had lodged with the Micawbers at their previous home in Windsor Terrace, off the City Road; but it was Dickens who remembered Camden Town as the home of 'faded gentility', of struggles with creditors, and indeed of John Dickens, the original for Mr Micawber. For Dickens, Camden Town remained associated with those traumatic first years in London.

THE 'POLYGON', CLARENDON SQUARE

Dickens returned to the area north of Bloomsbury a few years later. The Dickens family moved to Somers Town, first to 13 Johnson Street, and then, when Dickens was fifteen, to 17 the Polygon. The Polygon was the first housing to be built in Somers Town. It was a fifteen-sided arrangement of thirty-two houses, originally set among fields and gardens. Clarendon Square had been built around it by Dickens' day. The Polygon was pulled down in the 1890s, but it is remembered by the 'Polygon Road' that remains there.

When Dickens lived here, he worked as a solicitor's clerk, briefly for Charles Molloy and for over a year at Ellis and Blackmore in Gray's Inn. This experience reinforced in his mind the associations of Somers Town and Camden Town with the familiar presence of the 'clerk population' and he knew of their daily migrations by virtue of the fact that he had become part of the exodus.

Lowten, the solicitor Perker's clerk in *The Pickwick Papers*, walks through the Polygon to his place of work at Gray's Inn Square. One morning, Mr Pickwick is there to see him get there, anxiously concerned to arrive ahead of his employer:

The healthy light of a fine October morning made even the dingy old houses brighten up a little: some of the dusty windows actually looking almost cheerful as the sun's rays gleamed upon them. Clerk after clerk hastened into the square by one or other of the entrances, and looking up at the Hall clock, accelerated or decreased his rate of walking according to the time at which his office hours nominally commenced; the half-past nine o'clock people suddenly becoming very brisk, and the ten o'clock gentlemen falling into a pace of most aristocratic slowness. The clock struck ten, and clerks poured in faster than ever, each one in a greater perspiration than his predecessor. The noise of unlocking and opening doors echoed and re-echoed on every side, heads appeared as if by magic in every window, the porters took up their stations for the day, the slipshod laundresses hurried off, the postman ran from house to house, and the whole legal hive was in a bustle.

'You're early, Mr Pickwick,' said a voice behind him.

'Ah, Mr Lowten,' replied that gentleman, looking round, and recognizing his old acquaintance.

'Precious warm walking, isn't it?' said Lowten, drawing a Bramah key from his pocket, with a small plug therein, to keep the dust out.

'You appear to feel it so,' rejoined Mr Pickwick, smiling at the clerk, who was literally red hot.

'I've come along, rather, I can tell you,' replied Lowten. 'It went the half hour as I came through the Polygon. I'm here before him, though, so I don't mind.' (*PP*, 53)

The Polygon had originally attracted well-educated, middle-class inhabitants, including William Godwin and Mary Wollstonecraft. The area had already begun to deteriorate by the time that Dickens lived there, which made it more affordable to the lower middle classes. The construction and opening of the station and railway at Euston in 1838 accelerated the decline of the housing, until it was a faded remnant of its former attractiveness. Dickens' recollection of the Polygon was stamped with his distaste for false pretensions to wealth at exactly the time when he was striving to better himself. The 'faded gentility' that he remembered of his house in Bayham Street is matched by the 'shabby luxury' of Harold Skimpole's abode in the Polygon, in *Bleak House*:

> He lived in a place called the Polygon, in Somers Town, where there were at that time a number of poor Spanish refugees walking about in cloaks, smoking little paper cigars. Whether he was a better tenant than one might have supposed, in consequence of his friend Somebody always paying his rent at last, or whether his inaptitude for business rendered it particularly difficult to turn him out, I don't know; but he had occupied the same house some years. It was in a state of dilapidation quite equal to our expectation. Two or three of the area railings were gone; the water-butt was broken; the knocker was loose; the bell handle had been pulled off a long time, to judge from the rusty state of the wire; and dirty footprints on the steps were the only signs of its being inhabited. [...]
>
> We went up-stairs to the first floor, still seeing no other furniture than the dirty footprints. Mr. Jarndyce, without further ceremony, entered a room there, and we followed. It was dingy enough, and not at all clean; but furnished with an odd kind of shabby luxury, with a large footstool, a sofa, and plenty of cushions, an easy-chair, and plenty of pillows, a piano, books, drawing materials, music, newspapers, and a few sketches and pictures. A broken pane of glass in one of the dirty windows was papered and wafered over; but there was a little plate of hothouse nectarines on the table, and there was another of grapes, and another of sponge-cakes, and there was a bottle of light wine. Mr. Skimpole himself reclined upon the sofa, in a dressing-gown, drinking some fragrant coffee from an old china cup – it was then about midday – and looking at a collection of wallflowers in the balcony. (*BH*, 43)

The 'state of dilapidation' along with the pretensions to high comfort reflect Dickens' own recollections of living in the Polygon. They also reflect his experience of Somers Town and Camden Town generally. These were areas losing touch with their earlier grandeur, and it was not without some humiliation and embarrassment that Dickens recalled those days in which his family's poverty constrained them to the area.

LANT STREET

The most delicate memories of his childhood stem from the time when he worked at Warren's Blacking Factory. During these months in 1824, shortly before the family lived at the Polygon, Dickens moved from lodgings in Camden Town to lodgings at 1 Lant Street, in the Borough. From here, it was a short walk to the Marshalsea debtors' prison, where his father was incarcerated. Dickens went there daily, both for breakfast in the morning and for supper at night. Lant Street still runs between Southwark Bridge Road and Borough High Street, although the house has now gone. The house appears in *The Pickwick Papers* as Bob Sawyer's lodgings: 'Lant Street, Borough; it's near Guy's, and handy for me you know. Little distance after you've passed Saint George's Church – turns out of the High Street on the right hand side the way.' It was a poor area of London, and Dickens goes on to lampoon the uninspiring housing conditions, but despite its grim personal associations for him there is little hostility in his writing. The chapter in which Bob Sawyer hosts a bachelor party opens with a description of the street that is satiric but not embittered:

> There is a repose about Lant Street, in the Borough, which sheds a gentle melancholy upon the soul. There are always a good many houses to let in the street: it is a bye street too, and its dulness is soothing. A house in Lant Street would not come within the denomination of a first-rate residence, in the strict acceptation of the term; but it is a most desirable spot nevertheless. If a man wished to abstract himself from the

world; to remove himself from within the reach of temptation; to place himself beyond the possibility of any inducement to look out of the window, we should recommend him by all means to go to Lant Street.

In this happy retreat are colonized a few clear-starchers, a sprinkling of journeymen bookbinders, one or two prison agents for the Insolvent Court, several small housekeepers who are employed in the Docks, a handful of mantua-makers, and a seasoning of jobbing tailors. The majority of the inhabitants either direct their energies to the letting of furnished apartments, or devote themselves to the healthful and invigorating pursuit of mangling. The chief features in the still life of the street, are green shutters, lodging-bills, brass door-plates, and bell-handles; the principal specimens of animated nature, the pot-boy, the muffin youth, and the baked-potato man. The population is migratory, usually disappearing on the verge of quarter-day, and generally by night. His Majesty's revenues are seldom collected in this happy valley, the rents are dubious, and the water communication is very frequently cut off. (*PP*, 32)

The chapter begins by using the language of a romantic poet to describe Lant Street, which is ridiculous enough given the run-down state of the street, but all the more absurd bearing in mind that 'lant' was stale urine generally used for industrial purposes. Thereafter it has something of the wilful optimism of the estate agent, turning negatives into selling points. There are 'a good many houses to let in the street', which is not taken to be indicative of its undesirability, but as presenting an opportunity to the willing reader to move into the area. Its dullness is not a limiting factor, as it is deemed 'soothing', and the lack of any views is cast as the absence of distractions, of 'any inducement to look out of the window'. There is a cosmopolitan mix of employments, where 'the pot-boy, the muffin youth, and the baked-potato man' sounds like a sort of evolutionary development of a tradesman, or a working-class bildungsroman in miniature.

Dickens' writing about Lant Street was informed by his own experience as a lodger there. Although conditions were basic, the twelve year old Dickens was satisfied with the accommodation, and the move there had brought him closer to his family in the Marshalsea. The move had been a triumph for Dickens as he had

persuaded his father to move him there from the miserable
lodging in Little College Street that had compounded his
unhappiness when working at Warren's. Dickens recollects this
period in his 'Autobiographical Fragment':

> My rescue from this kind of existence I considered quite hopeless,
> and abandoned as such, altogether; though I am solemnly convinced
> that I never, for one hour, was reconciled to it, or was otherwise than
> miserably unhappy. I felt keenly, however, the being so cut off from
> my parents, my brothers, and sisters; and, when my day's work was
> done, going home to such a miserable blank; and that, I thought,
> might be corrected. One Sunday night I remonstrated with my father
> on this head, so pathetically and with so many tears, that his kind
> nature gave way. He began to think that it was not quite right. I do
> believe he had never thought so before, or thought about it. It was
> the first remonstrance I had ever made about my lot, and perhaps it
> opened up a little more than I intended. A back-attic was found for
> me at the house of an insolvent-court agent, who lived in Lant-street
> in the borough, where Bob Sawyer lodged many years afterwards.
> A bed and bedding were sent over for me, and made up on the floor.
> The little window had a pleasant prospect of a timber-yard; and when
> I took possession of my new abode, I thought it was a Paradise. (*AF*)

The house makes an appearance in *David Copperfield*, too. In this, Dickens' most autobiographical novel, David's reasons for moving into the house closely approximate those of Dickens. In fact, Dickens dovetails the words of his own recollection into David's. After Mr Micawber is sent to the King's Bench debtors' prison, itself a short walk from Lant Street, Mrs Micawber eventually decides to move with him, leaving David and the Orfling in search of new lodgings:

> a little room was hired outside the walls in the neighbourhood of that Institution, very much to my satisfaction, since the Micawbers and I had become too used to one another, in our troubles, to part. The Orfling was likewise accommodated with an inexpensive lodging in the same neighbourhood. Mine was a quiet back-garret with a sloping roof, commanding a pleasant prospect of a timber-yard; and when I took possession of it, with the reflection that Mr Micawber's troubles had come to a crisis at last, I thought it quite a paradise. (*DC*, 11)

Dickens' boyhood satisfaction with the place means that the lack of concern about the limited view, far from being the sham that it was in the *Pickwick Papers* extract, here reflects a cheerful willingness to make the best of his lot. Since his satisfaction with the simplicity of Lant Street owed much to his own circumstances, Dickens modifies his pleasure in David's version. The slight qualification he makes to, 'I thought it was a Paradise', turning it to 'I thought it quite a paradise', suggests that his own happiness with Lant Street, after persuading his father to find him a better and a closer lodging, does not translate comfortably to David's situation. So Dickens also inserts a justification for David's happy response to the property with the less convincing suggestion that he was glad 'that Mr Micawber's troubles had come to a crisis at last'.

FURNIVAL'S INN

A decade after Dickens had lived at Lant Street, and having occupied numerous lodgings in the meantime, he moved to Furnival's Inn. Furnival's Inn, on High Holborn, was one of the old Inns of Chancery. After 1817, it was no longer used for legal business, but rented out as lodgings, with part of it turned into hotel accommodation. Mr Grewgious, who lives across Holborn in Staple Inn (in *Edwin Drood*), takes his dinner there 'three hundred days in the year, at least', and he finds Rosa 'an airy, clean, comfortable, almost gay' room in the hotel. The building was demolished in 1897 but it is remembered by a tablet at the entrance of the present site, where Holborn Bars now stands.

Dickens moved there in 1834 and stayed for three years; it was there that he began to write *The Pickwick Papers*. Significantly for his later writing, it was also where he lived during much of his courting of Catherine Hogarth and for a short time after their marriage in 1836.

Looking back on the early days of Dickens' marriage with the knowledge of its later unhappiness and notoriously public breakdown, some writers have wondered whether he had been truly in love with Catherine or just believed himself to be so. That the comic farce about suspected adultery and marital miscommunication, *Is She His Wife?*, was finished when revisiting their honeymoon destination at Chalk is one potentially worrying indication. More reassuring are the happy associations that Furnival's Inn has in Dickens' fiction, and especially his choice to make it a setting in the developing romance of Ruth Pinch and John Westlock in *Martin Chuzzlewit* (1853–4).

First, it is the unusual configuration of the chambers within the Inn that gives it capital in Dickens' novel. When Tom Pinch goes to visit his old friend, John Westlock, in Furnival's Inn, he is confused by the layout of the building:

John Westlock lived in Furnival's Inn, High Holborn, which was within a quarter of an hour's walk of Tom's starting point, but seemed a long way off, by reason of his going two or three miles out of the straight road to make a short cut. When at last he arrived outside John's door, two stories up, he stood faltering with his hand upon the knocker [...].

Rat tat.

'I am afraid that's not a London knock,' thought Tom. 'It didn't sound bold. Perhaps that's the reason why nobody answers the door.'

It is quite certain that nobody came, and that Tom stood looking at the knocker: wondering whereabouts in the neighbourhood a certain gentleman resided, who was roaring out to somebody 'Come in!' with all his might.

'Bless my soul!' thought Tom at last. 'Perhaps he lives here, and is calling to me. I never thought of that. Can I open the door from the outside, I wonder. Yes, to be sure I can.'

To be sure he could, by turning the handle: and to be sure when he did turn it, the same voice came rushing out, crying 'Why don't you come in? Come in, do you hear? What are you standing there for?' quite violently.

Tom stepped from the little passage into the room from which these sounds proceeded. (*MC*, 36)

Presumably, Tom is knocking at the outer door of the passage leading to John Westlock's rooms, thinking it to be his front door, confused by the configuration of the chambers in the Inns which to this day are often grouped in clusters behind internal doors. A certain cachet attaches to an address at Furnival's Inn and Tom is nervous on his arrival there, partly for that reason. It soon works to his benefit though, when 'a reference from John Westlock, Esquire, Furnival's Inn, High Holborn' immediately helps Tom and his sister secure a lodging at short notice.

Perhaps Dickens himself took pride in his address at this time, when he was an aspiring writer wondering how his first novel was going to be received. The deepest influence of his experience of the Furnival's Inn rooms, however, is evident when it becomes the scene of a developing romance between John Westlock and Ruth Pinch. One evening, while Tom plays on the piano, John and Ruth sit at the window seat and look out into the twilight:

> There is little enough to see, in Furnival's Inn. It is a shady, quiet place, echoing to the footsteps of the stragglers who have business there; and rather monotonous and gloomy on summer evenings. What gave it such a charm to them, that they remained at the window as unconscious of the flight of time as Tom himself, the dreamer, while the melodies which had so often soothed his spirit, were hovering again about him! What power infused into the fading light, the gathering darkness; the stars that here and there appeared; the evening air, the city's hum and stir, the very chiming of the old church clocks; such exquisite enthralment, that the divinest regions of the earth spread out before their eyes could not have held them captive in a stronger chain!
>
> The shadows deepened; deepened; and the room became quite dark. Still Tom's fingers wandered over the keys of the piano; and still the window had its pair of tenants. (*MC*, 45)

The dullness of the inn, 'rather monotonous and gloomy', offers a counterpoint to the increasing interest and excitement of the romance. As the next chapter of this book shows, the

Inns of Chancery and the Inns of Court are often associated in Dickens' mind and writing with the loneliness of bachelors. His own experience of courting Catherine Hogarth whilst living in Furnival's Inn sharpened the sense of contrast between the lonely, gloomy inns and the happiness of private love, which infuses this passage in *Martin Chuzzlewit*. That sense of contrast that Dickens felt for himself when he lived there can be glimpsed in some of his other writing about Legal London.

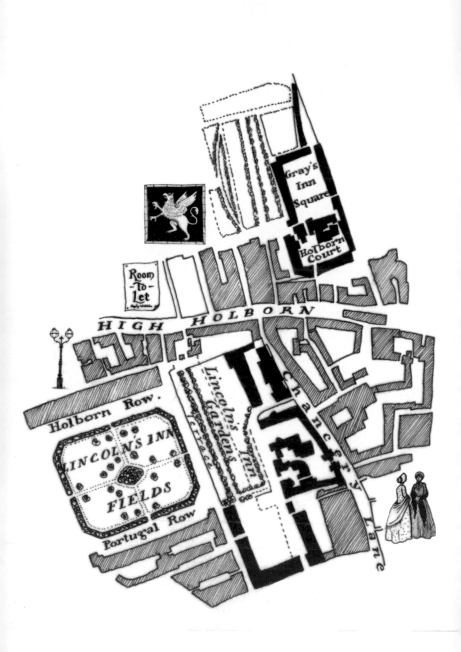

LEGAL LONDON

ondon's historic Inns of Court and Inns of Chancery had
long been home to the city's legal profession. The four Inns
of Court were, as they still are, professional associations of
barristers, with their own premises in London's central legal
area. These are Lincoln's Inn, Inner Temple, Middle Temple and
Gray's Inn. There were also nine Inns of Chancery, which
provided associations and offices for solicitors. They included
Staple Inn, Furnival's Inn, Clifford's Inn, Clement's Inn, New
Inn and Barnard's Inn. By the time of Dickens' writing, other
associations for solicitors existed; the Inns of Chancery were
becoming redundant, and they soon fell into decline. None of
them are still functioning today, although the premises of Staple
Inn remain. The Inns of Court and Chancery each offered a
dining hall, a library, a chapel and professional accommodation,
all arranged around garden courtyards. Each was comprised of
'chambers' which were intended as professional offices but by
Dickens' day were increasingly being used as accommodation.
The Court of Chancery was then housed at Westminster Hall,
before moving to the Royal Courts of Justice in 1882.[1]

The Inns feature frequently in Dickens' writing and numerous
of his characters live or lodge at chambers in one Inn or
another. Dickens characterised them as dry, dusty, dilapidated
places, providing accommodation for bachelors. This view of
them emerges in many of his novels, but it is in a zany sketch in
the *Uncommercial Traveller* papers that he puts it most directly.
Chambers are unimaginative, soulless places, because no families
have ever lived there, no romances have taken place there, no
children have learned to read there:

> It is to be remarked of chambers in general, that they must have been
> built for chambers, to have the right kind of loneliness. You may make a
> great dwelling-house very lonely, by isolating suites of rooms and calling

them chambers, but you cannot make the true kind of loneliness. In dwelling-houses, there have been family festivals; children have grown in them, girls have bloomed into women in them, courtships and marriages have taken place in them. True chambers were never young, childish, maidenly; never had dolls in them, or rocking-horses, or christenings, or betrothals, or little coffins. Let Gray's Inn identify the child who first touched hands and hearts with Robinson Crusoe, in any one of its many 'sets,' and that child's little statue, in white marble with a golden inscription, shall be at its service, at my cost and charge, as a drinking fountain for the spirit, to freshen its thirsty square. Let Lincoln's produce from all its houses, a twentieth of the procession derivable from any dwelling-house one-twentieth of its age, of fair young brides who married for love and hope, not settlements, and all the Vice-Chancellors shall thence-forward be kept in nosegays for nothing, on application to the writer hereof. ('Chambers', *UT*)

Dickens' writing about places in London frequently attends, as this book shows, to the buried histories, the historical associations, connected to the place. This is true of his writing about chambers, or 'sets' as the collections of rooms were also known. Throughout his oeuvre, they are forever stamped with the loneliness of the bachelors who have lived there. They are weirdly fancy-free places because they are homes that have never housed families, loves, children or imaginations. Dickens, as the Uncommercial Traveller, promises to erect statues in the squares of the Inns as drinking fountains, and to supply the vice-chancellors with flowers, if anything can be shown to the contrary.

STAPLE INN

The grubby state of many of the Inns in the nineteenth century significantly influenced the way that Dickens perceived them. To other eyes, they were not as barren and sterile as he made out, owing especially to the lawns that many of them contained. Throughout his writing career, Dickens acknowledges the unusual topography of the Inns and their associated chambers. They were typically built around garden quadrangles, in the manner of the colleges of Oxford and Cambridge, providing a rural retreat in the middle of a dense city.

But the state of many of these Inns of Court was so dilapidated, that their pretensions to offer secluded country-like gardens within the heart of the city were unconvincing for Dickens. This was especially true of Staple Inn. In *Bleak House*, Dickens pokes fun at Mr Snagsby's delusions about London's pastoral nooks, which give him such 'a flavour of the country' that he does not need to experience the real thing. Mr Snagsby is 'in his way, rather a meditative and poetical man', and so he loves 'to walk in Staple Inn in the summer time, and to observe how countrified the sparrows and the leaves are' (*BH*, 10).

In Dickens' day, Staple Inn had become little more than a
social club for lawyers, rather than the legal training college that
it had once been. It still stands today in High Holborn. It is one
of London's few surviving Tudor buildings and it features a
distinctive black and white timber facade that recalls its origins.
In *The Mystery of Edwin Drood* (1865), Mr Grewgious, a lawyer
and a bachelor, occupies chambers at Staple Inn. The Inn's
antiquity combined with its pastoral pretensions reminded
Dickens that in ancient times a small brook, known as the 'Old
Bourne' and from which 'Holborn' allegedly takes its name, ran
through the area and into the nearby River Fleet:

Behind the most ancient part of Holborn, London, where certain
gabled houses some centuries of age still stand looking on the public
way, as if disconsolately looking for the Old Bourne that has long run
dry, is a little nook composed of two irregular quadrangles, called
Staple Inn. It is one of those nooks, the turning into which out of the
clashing street, imparts to the relieved pedestrian the sensation of

having put cotton in his ears, and velvet soles on his boots. It is one of those nooks where a few smoky sparrows twitter in smoky trees, as though they called to one another, 'Let us play at country,' and where a few feet of garden mould and a few yards of gravel enable them to do that refreshing violence to their tiny understandings. Moreover, it is one of those nooks which are legal nooks; and it contains a little Hall, with a little lantern in its roof: to what obstructive purposes devoted, and at whose expense, this history knoweth not. (*ED*, 11)

The description takes the peaceful, secluded garden, the boast of many of the Inns, with little seriousness. The birds that inhabit the scene are merely sparrows – town birds that give only the most meagre approximation to countryside wildlife. The unknown 'obstructive purposes' to which the lantern is devoted suggests another reason why Dickens has such little truck with the apparent attractions of the Inns – he was so thoroughly resentful of the injustice that he thought the legal profession as it then existed was set up to perpetuate.

BARNARD'S INN

When Pip first arrives in London in pursuit of his great expectations, he takes up lodgings at Barnard's Inn, the other of the Inns of Chancery (with Staple Inn) to be associated with Gray's Inn. Much of Barnard's Inn has since been demolished, but the old Hall still remains, as part of Gresham College in Holborn, a short walk east from Staple Inn. As they walk there, Pip is disappointed to find that Wemmick does not hold him in especially high regard on account of his expectations. Wemmick then says that they have arrived:

My depression was not alleviated by the announcement, for, I had supposed that establishment to be an hotel kept by Mr. Barnard, to which the Blue Boar in our town was a mere public-house. Whereas I now found Barnard to be a disembodied spirit, or a fiction, and his inn the dingiest collection of shabby buildings ever squeezed together in a rank corner as a club for Tomcats.

We entered this haven through a wicket-gate, and were disgorged by an introductory passage into a melancholy little square that looked to me like a flat burying-ground. I thought it had the most dismal trees in it, and the most dismal sparrows, and the most dismal cats, and the most dismal houses (in number half a dozen or so), that I had ever seen. I thought the windows of the sets of chambers into which these houses were divided, were in every stage of dilapidated blind and curtain, crippled flower-pot, cracked glass, dusty decay, and miserable makeshift; while To Let To Let To Let, glared at me from empty rooms, as if no new wretches ever came there, and the vengeance of the soul of Barnard were being slowly appeased by the gradual suicide of the present occupants and their unholy interment under the gravel. A frouzy mourning of soot and smoke attired this forlorn creation of Barnard, and it had strewn ashes on its head, and was undergoing penance and humiliation as a mere dust-hole. Thus far my sense of sight; while dry rot and wet rot and all the silent rots that rot in neglected roof and cellar – rot of rat and mouse and bug and coaching-stables near at hand besides – addressed themselves faintly to my sense of smell, and moaned, 'Try Barnard's Mixture.'

So imperfect was this realization of the first of my great expectations, that I looked in dismay at Mr. Wemmick. 'Ah!' said he, mistaking me; 'the retirement reminds you of the country. So it does me.' (*GE* II, 2)

This is an important episode in Pip's progress because it represents the first disappointment of his expectations. Long before Pip realises that Miss Havisham is not his benefactor as he had dreamed, or that Estella is not intended for him, his arrival at Barnard's Inn, which he had wrongly anticipated to be a comfortable hotel, creates a climate of disappointment that extends throughout the novel and alerts readers that Pip's hopes may survive only to be dashed.

The chapter was published in Dickens' own journal, *All the Year Round*, in February 1861, just months after his paper on 'Chambers' had appeared in the same publication in August 1860. Dickens' description of Barnard's Inn borrows from the earlier piece, at least in its tone and general attitude towards chambers. The images of dust and decay, the suspicion of suicide, and the sepulchral atmosphere of the courtyard, are common to both passages, although the witty personification of 'Barnard' is unique to the novel.

LINCOLN'S INN

Bleak House is the novel that most fully involves one of the Inns of Court. Lincoln's Inn is at the heart of the protracted action of the novel, or as the opening paragraph has it, 'at the heart of the fog'. Dickens knew the surrounding area well. He lived for many years in houses in nearby streets and his great friend, John Forster, lived in Lincoln's Inn Fields, the garden square on the outside of the Inn's walls. It was at Forster's home that Dickens first read his second Christmas book, *The Chimes*. The streets in the vicinity of the Inn play host to many of the novel's events. Tulkinghorn is murdered in his house in Lincoln's Inn Fields and Krook's shop, where Krook spontaneously combusts and where the Jarndyce will is ultimately found, is propped against the walls of the Inn.

Lincoln's Inn itself dates back to the fourteenth century. Its outer wall, separating its buildings and courtyards from the surrounding streets, was built subsequently in 1562. The Inn is located in Holborn, at the centre of London's legal district. Chancery Lane runs along its eastern perimeter. Lincoln's Inn comprises squares such as Old Square, Stone Buildings and New Square. It has a chapel (in which John Donne was once the preacher), a library and a Great Hall. *Bleak House* famously opens here: 'London. Michaelmas Term lately over, and the Lord Chancellor sitting in Lincoln's Inn Hall' (*BH*, 1).

Esther meets Richard and Ada when she is summoned to Lincoln's Inn by the Lord Chancellor. The solicitors Kenge and Carboy have their offices there. Esther goes to these offices immediately before being called before the Lord Chancellor:

> We drove slowly through the dirtiest and darkest streets that ever were seen in the world (I thought), and in such a distracting state of confusion that I wondered how the people kept their senses, until we passed into sudden quietude under an old gateway, and drove on through a silent square until we came to an odd nook in a corner, where there was an entrance up a steep broad flight of stairs, like an entrance to a church. And there really was a church-yard, outside under some cloisters, for I saw the gravestones from the staircase window.
>
> This was Kenge and Carboy's. (*BH*, 3)

Dickens' depiction of Lincoln's Inn is of a dark and dreary set of buildings where youth and hope are seldom present. The eccentric old lady Miss Flite puts it most often in these abstract terms, when she says, wrily: 'It is a good omen for youth, and hope, and beauty, when they find themselves in this place, and don't know what's to come of it' (*BH*, 3), and she continues to emphasise the incongruity of the presence of 'youth, and hope, and beauty' amid the confines of Lincoln's Inn.

Esther recognises the contrast as she looks admiringly at Ada Clare, when she meets her at Lincoln's Inn:

> It touched me, that the home of such a beautiful young creature should be represented by that dry official place. The Lord High Chancellor, at his best, appeared so poor a substitute for the love and pride of parents. (*BH*, 3)

The contrast between the love and pride of family life and the dry, official Inns of Court, is one that Dickens highlights in his essay on 'Chambers' and exploits throughout his fiction.

Dickens reworks the theme in the case of Bart Smallweed. Instead of drawing a contrast between his youth and the surroundings of Lincoln's Inn, the grandson of the money-lender, Grandfather Smallweed, is first described amid the Inn as never having had a childhood:

> Whether Young Smallweed ... was ever a boy, is much doubted in Lincoln's Inn. He is now something under fifteen, and an old limb of the law. He is facetiously understood to entertain a passion for a lady at a cigar shop, in the neighbourhood of Chancery Lane, and for her sake to have broken off a contract with another lady, to whom he had been engaged some years. ... He is honoured with Mr Guppy's particular confidence, and occasionally advises him, from the deep wells of his experience, on difficult points in private life. (*BH*, 20)

Characteristically of the Inns of Court throughout Dickens' writing, Lincoln's Inn throws into strong relief the presence of any youthful virtues that are able to survive there.

GRAY'S INN

Although Dickens knew Lincoln's Inn well, he was even more closely familiar with Gray's Inn. He was an articled clerk there from May 1827 to late 1828, when he worked for the firm Ellis and Blackmore. Names such as Weller, Bardell and Rudge, which Dickens was later to use, are found in the firm's petty cash book, now kept in America.

Mr Perker, the attorney enlisted by Mr Pickwick to support him against Dodson and Fogg in the breach of promise case brought by Mrs Bardell, has chambers at Gray's Inn. When Mr Pickwick first calls, Perker has left for the day, so he tracks down his clerk, Lowten, at a local tavern, where he attempts to stimulate conversation with Lowten and his companions by saying: 'I have been to-night in a place which you all know very well, doubtless, but which I have not been in before, for some years, and know very little of; I mean Gray's Inn, gentlemen. Curious little nooks in a great place, like London, these old inns are.' Mr Pickwick's attempt to stimulate conversation has ominous repercussions as one of their number, old Jack Bamber, 'was never heard to talk about anything else but the Inns, and he has lived alone in them, till he's half crazy'.

The strange man's stories, in chapter 21 of the novel, are a prototype of Dickens' later *Uncommercial Traveller* paper, 'Chambers'. He relates a series of anecdotes connected to legal chambers, which are places full of gothic mystery and long, grim pasts. He thinks of the students who have laboured away in such rooms, and grown old there; and of the plaintiffs who have brought their suits there, often without success:

> They are no ordinary houses, those. There is not a panel in the old wainscotting, but what, if it were endowed with the powers of speech and memory, could start from the wall, and tell its tale of horror – the romance of life, Sir, the romance of life! Common-place as they may seem now, I tell you they are strange old places, and I would rather hear many a legend with a terrific-sounding name, than the true history of one old set of chambers. (*PP*, 21)

In the 'Chambers' paper, it is Gray's Inn that prompts most of the stories that are told. Dickens savages Gray's Inn itself:

> Indeed, I look upon Gray's Inn generally as one of the most depressing institutions in brick and mortar, known to the children of men. Can anything be more dreary than its arid Square, Sahara Desert of the law, with the ugly old tiled-topped tenements, the dirty windows, the bills To Let, To Let, the door-posts inscribed like gravestones, the crazy gateway giving upon the filthy Lane, the scowling iron-barred prison-like passage into Verulam-buildings, the mouldy red-nosed ticket-porters with little coffin plates, and why with aprons, the dry hard atomy-like appearance of the whole dust heap? When my uncommercial travels tend to this dismal spot, my comfort is its rickety state. Imagination gloats over the fullness of time when the staircases shall have quite tumbled down. ('Chambers', *UT*)

Throughout Dickens' writing career, the Inns of Court are associated for him with loneliness and often death. The limited appeal of their gardens is no match in Dickens' eyes for the dusty, dirty, dilapidated conditions of the buildings, nor for the oddity of the private histories of the chambers, where men have lived and laboured in isolation to the point of eccentricity. It was Gray's Inn that came to his mind more quickly than any other place when he wanted a specific Inn to lambast.

But in *David Copperfield*, Dickens goes some way to alleviate the grim associations that Gray's Inn had for him. A short time after Dora's death, David leaves England for Europe, where he spends three years recovering his health and his spirits. But on his return home, he goes immediately to visit Traddles who has by this time taken chambers at Gray's Inn. Everything about the Inn, its 'stiff-necked, long-established, solemn, elderly air', even the imposing furniture, makes David thoroughly despondent about Traddles' chances of making a successful living in the law. In this frame of mind, he climbs the staircase to Traddles' chambers, tripping up on the way. On his approach, he hears sounds that seem out of place amid the staid atmosphere of the legal chambers:

In the course of my stumbling up-stairs, I fancied I heard a pleasant sound of laughter; and not the laughter of an attorney or barrister, or attorney's clerk or barrister's clerk, but of two or three merry girls. Happening, however, as I stopped to listen, to put my foot in a hole where the Honourable Society of Gray's Inn had left a plank deficient, I fell down with some noise, and when I recovered my footing all was silent. (*DC*, 59)

This is an odd mix of legal satire and slapstick, as if the hero of this realist novel is in danger of becoming a pantomime clown.

When David is shown into Traddles' rooms, everything seems to be in order. His friend is sitting behind his desk, bending over some papers, though David notices he is suspiciously out of breath. The two share a joyful reunion, in the course of which Traddles reveals that he is married to Sophy, 'the dearest girl in the world':

'Why, my dear boy, she's behind the window-curtain! Look here!'
    To my amazement, the dearest girl in the world came at that same instant, laughing and blushing, from her place of concealment. (*DC*, 59)

Not only that, but Sophy's sisters are staying with the newly-weds, as they 'have come to have a peep at London', and they are hiding in the next room:

'[W]hen you tumbled up-stairs,' said Traddles, 'I was romping with the girls. In point of fact, we were playing at Puss in the Corner. But as that wouldn't do in Westminster Hall, and as it wouldn't look quite professional if they were seen by a client, they decamped.' (*DC,* 59)

Traddles tells David about each of the sisters, one by one, and how they are being innovatively looked after with minimal resources by his new wife.

'Now the whole set – I mean the chambers – is only three rooms; but Sophy arranges for the girls in the most wonderful way, and they sleep as comfortably as possible. Three in that room,' said Traddles, pointing. 'Two in that.' (*DC*, 59)

The joke at the start of this quotation is that 'the whole set' might be a casual reference to all of the sisters, until Traddles clarifies that he is using 'set' in its technical sense to refer to his chambers. It extends the odd juxtaposition of the legal and the playful in this scene into the language itself. The same is true of the earlier sentence: 'In point of fact, we were playing at Puss in the Corner', where the formal, legal, turn of phrase, 'in point of fact', introduces Traddles' ridiculous confession. In Dickens' next novel, *Bleak House*, he would exploit a similar equivocation in the word 'suitors', when describing the vicinity of Lincoln's Inn during the long vacation, playing host to 'a tenderer class of suitors than is usually found there' (*BH*, 19). Dickens was able to find in legal vocabulary suggestions of more romantic, playful possibilities than were usually associated with the dry, dusty chambers. It was these possibilities, glaringly incongruous within the arid atmosphere of professional law, that he was beginning to resurrect in describing Traddles' residence at Gray's Inn. He was redeeming those chambers from all the associations of loneliness and bachelordom that his own writing had established for them. Traddles observes that excited female laughter was very 'agreeable to hear' in the chambers, as a point of contrast with the severity of the antique rooms:

> It quite lights up these old rooms. To an unfortunate bachelor of a fellow who has lived alone all his life, you know, it's positively delicious. It's charming. Poor things, they have had a great loss in Sophy – who, I do assure you, Copperfield, is, and ever was, the dearest girl! – and it gratifies me beyond expression to find them in such good spirits. The society of girls is a very delightful thing, Copperfield. It's not professional, but it's very delightful. (*DC,* 59)

The fulfilment of Traddles' hope and happiness, and even the deliverance of Gray's Inn itself, is significant in its place in the novel, because it quietly rebuts David's own despondency and sets the reader in mind, as the novel moves towards its conclusion, that the future may not be as bleak for David as he presently fears. Traddles' delighted remarks about the new light in which his rooms are now seen contains one further subtle turn of the jargon of the legal profession to new, more 'delicious' and 'charming' ends, as the 'Honourable Society of Grays' Inn' has become, against all precedent, a place for Traddles to enjoy 'the society of girls'.

CLEMENT'S INN

The imaginative energy associated with the legal Inns in Dickens' fiction is almost exclusively provided by his own writing. The only trace of imaginative life he observes in the Inns in reality is connected to the sundial in the gardens at Clement's Inn. Clement's Inn, located near St Clement Danes, on the south-east corner of the site now occupied by the Royal Courts of Justice, was the last of the Inns of Chancery to be closed. It shut in 1903. Until they were demolished in 1888, the Clement's Inn gardens featured the distinctive statue of a young African, kneeling and holding a sundial flat above his head. The statue can now be found in King's Bench Walk, in the Inner Temple. Dickens reports, with little enthusiasm, the legend associated with the sundial:

> The only popular legend known in relation to any one of the dull family of Inns, is a dark Old Bailey whisper concerning Clement's, and importing how the black creature who holds the sun-dial there, was a negro who slew his master and built the dismal pile out of the contents of his strong box – for which architectural offence alone he ought to have been condemned to live in it. But, what populace would waste fancy upon such a place, or on New Inn, Staple Inn, Barnard's Inn, or any of the shabby crew? ('Chambers', *UT*)

The sundial stands as an intrusion of the imagination within the grounds of the dark and dismal Inn. Dickens' subsequent claim in the paper that he would erect a statue, as a drinking fountain, in the square of any Inn where a child had encountered Robinson Crusoe, would provide a monument to the imagination in a manner that parallels Clement's Inn's strange sundial. While intended to convey the improbability of the occurrence, the anticipated statue suggests how Dickens relished the appearance of imagination, of youth and hope and beauty, within the precincts of the Inns, the same impetus that lay behind the contrast he drew between the old rooms and the youthful girlish laughter in *David Copperfield*.

FOUNTAIN COURT, MIDDLE TEMPLE

The sense of contrast provided by the sundial, or the statue, or even the nosegays for the vice-chancellors, elicits the artistic resonances of the fountain in Fountain Court, in Middle Temple, which features prominently in *Martin Chuzzlewit*. There it is a focal point for the love story between Ruth Pinch and John Westlock.

Late in the novel, when Tom Pinch has taken up mysterious employment in the Temple, he arranges to meet his sister after work, and their place of meeting is typically Fountain Court. Dickens writes most evocatively about this meeting place in the chapter in which it is not first Tom that she meets, but, catching her by surprise, her prospective lover, John Westlock.

At this point, Dickens' prose stages a sympathetic rivalry between Ruth and the fountain. She arrives 'with the best little laugh upon her face that ever played in opposition to the fountain, and beat it all to nothing'. The parallels between the 'sparkling' girl and the fountain with a pool where 'dimples sparkled on its sunny face' catalyses Dickens' writing:

> Whether there was life enough left in the slow vegetation of Fountain Court for the smoky shrubs to have any consciousness of the brightest and purest-hearted little woman in the world, is a question for gardeners, and those who are learned in the loves of plants. But, that it was a good thing for that same paved yard to have such a delicate little figure flitting through it; that it passed like a smile from the grimy old houses, and the worn flagstones, and left them duller, darker, sterner than before; there is no sort of doubt. The Temple fountain might have leaped up twenty feet to greet the spring of hopeful maidenhood, that in her person stole on, sparkling, through the dry and dusty channels of the Law; the chirping sparrows, bred in Temple chinks and crannies, might have held their peace to listen to imaginary skylarks, as so fresh a little creature passed; the dingy boughs, unused to droop, otherwise than in their puny growth, might have bent down in a kindred gracefulness, to shed their benedictions on her graceful head; old love letters, shut up in iron boxes in the neighbouring offices, and made of no account among the heaps of family papers into which they had strayed, and of which, in their degeneracy, they formed a part, might have stirred and fluttered with a moment's recollection of their ancient tenderness, as she went lightly by. Anything might have happened that did not happen, and never will, for the love of Ruth. (*MC*, 45)

The poetry of Dickens' style is strikingly evident in this passage. The sentence beginning 'The Temple fountain might have leaped up twenty feet to greet the spring of hopeful maidenhood' falls into an iambic rhythm, impelled by the internal

rhyme of 'feet' and 'greet'. There are numerous other rhymes
and chimes ('shed … head', 'unused to droop', which also
anticipates the passage's final word and prevailing spirit, 'Ruth').
The prose is full of alliterative patterns ('duller, darker', 'dry and
dusty', 'channels … chirping … chinks'). By the sequence of 'i'
sounds in 'delicate little figure flitting through it' Dickens
creates the image of Ruth tripping quickly through Fountain
Court. This is to say that, in this acoustically rich prose, Dickens
provides the poetry that the Inns of Court ordinarily lack.

Even if the imagined reanimation of Fountain Court does not
happen, though it 'might have happened', and Ruth's visit, like a
'passing smile', leaves the place 'duller, darker, sterner than before',
the conjectures of Inner Temple being enlivened raise the possibility of the Inn's redemption from dilapidation and degradation.
Ruth's presence is nevertheless seen as 'a good thing' for the yard.
The love scene does not fail to improve this part of Middle Temple
for the better. Already the 'chirping sparrows' seem more cheerful
than the 'smoky sparrows' of Staple Inn, or the 'dismal sparrows' of
Barnard's Inn. And ever after this point, the fountain itself seems
wakened into bonds of sympathy with Ruth and her suitor:

> Merrily the tiny fountain played, and merrily the dimples sparkled on
> its sunny face. John Westlock hurried after her. Softly the whispering
> water broke and fell; and roguishly the dimples twinkled; as he stole
> upon her footsteps. (*MC*, 45)

Though Ruth was previously described as 'sparkling', as I have
noted, here it is the dimples in the fountain pool that 'sparkled'.
In passages where Dickens hams up the contrived happenstance
of this meeting and his novel plays dumb about the growing
love between Ruth and John Westlock, the narrative voice
displaces its attention onto the fountain itself, but with its
merry play, its twinkling roguish dimples, and its soft whisper-
ing, we get enough sense of the scene taking place between
Ruth and John.

As the fountain becomes a refrain in this chapter, it becomes
imbued with more of Ruth's happy characteristics:

Merrily the fountain plashed and plashed, until the dimples, merging into one another, swelled into a general smile, that covered the whole surface of the basin. (*MC*, 45)

Ruth's visit seemed to pass 'like a smile' across the buildings of the Temple, and now a 'general smile' forms in the basin of the fountain. And then it breaks into a laugh to match the 'little laugh' that Ruth gave as she arrived at Fountain Court:

Merrily the fountain leaped and danced, and merrily the smiling dimples twinkled and expanded more and more, until they broke into a laugh against the basin's rim, and vanished. *(MC*, 45)

By the end of the novel, the transformation of Fountain Court has taken hold. Although Dickens would write again and again about the dismal environs of London's legal heartland, of the gloomy and dilapidated Inns of Court and of Chancery, in *Martin Chuzzlewit* as in *David Copperfield*, he recognised that they could be redeemed for the better by love and imagination, virtues that Dickens felt the Inns had so long been without:

Brilliantly the Temple Fountain sparkled in the sun, and laughingly its liquid music played, and merrily the idle drops of water danced and danced, and peeping out in sport among the trees, plunged lightly down to hide themselves, as little Ruth and her companion came towards it. (*MC*, 53)

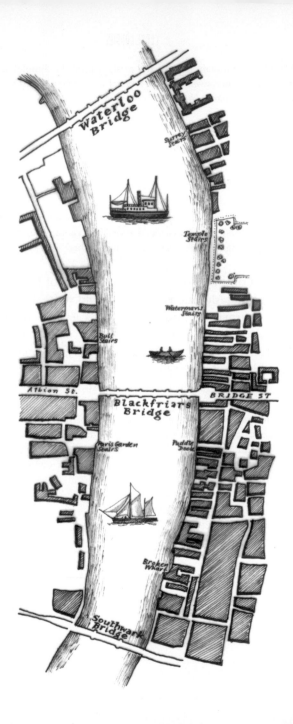

THE RIVER AND ITS BRIDGES

London Bridge was the only bridge across the Thames in the city until the eighteenth century. When Dickens was born, the river in central London was crossed only by London, Westminster and Blackfriars bridges. Vauxhall, Waterloo and Southwark bridges were all added in the second decade of the nineteenth century to meet the rising demand and also to make a tidy profit through the imposition of tolls.

The construction of half the city's bridges in the years prior to Dickens beginning his writing career impressed them onto his imagination, as did his own familiarity with them from walking across them regularly throughout his life. They provide him with ways to date the action of his fiction. Several of his novels are explicitly set before the construction of the new London Bridge in 1832. More than this, Dickens' imagination responded to the bridges as unique combinations of fixity and movement. On the one hand, the bridges were massive, solid constructions. They were built to last, best exemplified by the 800-year history of the old London Bridge. On the other hand, they crossed a river that was ever-changing, ever-flowing out to sea. Some of the bridges were so busy that the passage of people and vehicles across them was equally swift and rapid. In that case too, there was a striking contrast between the busy city traffic and the more peaceful perspectives of the wide river.

This combination of stasis and flux, of bustle and rest, plays into Dickens' writing about the bridges. Sometimes his characters go there alone and in contemplative moods, either to gaze upon the roofs and spires that are visible or to watch the ever-moving river below them. The bridges provide visible metaphors, as it were, for his characters' calm demeanours beneath which flows a more turbulent inner life. In these cases, the river takes on its own set of resonances, variously symbolising freedom, echoes of eternity, even inevitable death.

The bridges are also often the site of planned meetings or chance encounters. As the expanding city funnelled more and more people across its bridges, they converged at these crossing points in ways that they didn't throughout the rest of the city. The bridges are specifically designed for crossing, of course, for moving on, and yet they are also meeting places, and places to stop. Dickens responds to all these attributes of London's bridges, with the effect that they can be both pauses and springs of action in his fiction.

WATERLOO BRIDGE

Designed by John Rennie, Waterloo Bridge was constructed of granite, with nine arches linking its stone columns. Named to commemorate the British victory at the Battle of Waterloo in 1815, the bridge opened in 1817. A toll was charged as it was one of the bridges built and owned by private companies as a profit-making enterprise. The fee remained until the bridge was nationalised when it was bought by the Metropolitan Board of Works in 1878. The toll ensured that vehicles and foot passengers remained at a low level. In strong contrast to the crowding of Blackfriars and London bridges, Dickens was struck by the tranquillity of Waterloo Bridge.

In *Little Dorrit*, Arthur Clennam follows Miss Wade and Tattycoram down the Strand. When they arrive at the Adelphi, which is just downriver of Waterloo Bridge, Dickens comments on the peacefulness of the place:

> There is always, to this day, a sudden pause in that place to the roar of the great thoroughfare. The many sounds become so deadened that the change is like putting cotton in the ears, or having the head thickly muffled. At that time the contrast was far greater; there being no small steam boats on the river, no landing-places but slippery wooden stairs and foot-causeways, no railroad on the opposite bank, no hanging bridge or fish-market near at hand, no traffic on the nearest bridge of stone, nothing moving on the stream but watermen's wherries and coal-lighters. (*LD*, II, 9)

The lack of traffic on 'the nearest bridge of stone', namely Waterloo Bridge, is likely to have been because the toll dissuaded people from using it. The bridge is part of a scene of unusual quietness in a busy city. It is a characteristic of Dickens' writing about bridges, that they are locations of peacefulness for his characters. This is especially so of Southwark Bridge, for which a toll was also levied and which provides *Little Dorrit* with opportunities for quiet contemplation. To a degree it is also true of the much busier bridges, including Blackfriars and London bridges, which still offer tranquil perspectives of the river and several of Dickens' characters pause on these bridges too.

BLACKFRIARS BRIDGE

Dickens knew Blackfriars Bridge well because he usually crossed it on the way back to his lodgings in Lant Street when working at the blacking factory. Completed in 1768, it was the third bridge across the Thames in the centre of London. It was demolished in 1864, when a new bridge was designed and built. Unlike the newer bridges, Waterloo downstream and Southwark upstream, no charge was levied to use Blackfriars and it was consequently extremely busy in the years that Dickens knew it. The crowd of people hurrying past is a feature of Dickens' description when Jo, the crossing-sweep in *Bleak House*, is moved on there. So too is the view. The bridge offered one of the most striking views of the dome of St Paul's in all of London:

> Jo moves on, through the long vacation, down to Blackfriars Bridge where he finds a baking stony corner, wherein to settle his repast.
>
> And there he sits, munching and gnawing, and looking up at the great Cross on the summit of St Paul's Cathedral, glittering above a red and violet-tinted cloud of smoke. From the boy's face one might suppose that sacred emblem to be, in his eyes, the crowning confusion of the great, confused city; so golden, so high up, so far out of his reach. There he sits, the sun going down, the river running fast, the crowd flowing by him in two streams – everything moving on to some purpose and to one end until he is stirred up, and told to 'move on' too. (*BH*, 19)

London's bridges, with their solid structures crossing the ever-flowing river, often presented to Dickens' imagination a striking contrast between stasis and movement. That contrast is activated by this passage, as Jo arrives at Blackfriars Bridge. Dickens presents the scene with these competing claims of stasis and movement in mind. Jo sits down in the corner of the bridge and his brief rest is contrasted with the sinking sun, the flowing river and the hurrying crowds. Dickens' chosen idiom as Jo eats the food that Mr Snagsby has given him – 'to settle his repast' – enhances the sense of settling down. But everything seems caught up with the movement suggested by the Thames. Even the crowd is described as 'flowing by him in two streams', taking on the characteristics of the rushing river. The same can be said of a moment in *David Copperfield*, when David follows Martha into the vicinity of Westminster Bridge. She is able to proceed quickly, once 'she got free of the two currents of passengers setting towards and from the bridge' (*DC*, 47). The river passing underneath the bridges provides Dickens with a model of movement that influences the way he sees the numbers of people coming to and from the bridges. For Jo, seeking rest amid this torrent of activity, he is 'stirred up, and told to "move on" too', as if he has been caught in a current.

LONDON BRIDGE

When Dickens worked in the blacking factory, before work each day he would join his father, confined in the Marshalsea, for breakfast. Until the gates opened, he would loiter 'in his lounging place by London-bridge'. This becomes David Copperfield's habit while waiting for the gates to open at the King's Bench Prison, where Mr Micawber had been taken an inmate. London Bridge was one of the city's major thoroughfares and it was often extremely congested. By the late nineteenth century, 22,000 vehicles and 110,000 pedestrians crossed it every day.[1] David finds it a pleasant retreat nonetheless:

> I forget, too, at what hour the gates were opened in the morning, admitting of my going in; but I know that I was often up at six o'clock, and that my favourite lounging-place in the interval was old London Bridge, where I was wont to sit in one of the stone recesses, watching the people going by. (*DC*, 11)

This was old London Bridge, as David says, which had existed in this form since its last redevelopment in 1762. Originally built in 1176 as the first stone bridge across the Thames, it was replaced by the new, five-arched granite bridge in 1831. In one of the *Sketches by Boz*, 'Scotland Yard', Dickens writes about the arrival of the new bridge from the cynical, suspicious perspectives of coal-heavers in that area of London, a downtrodden part of Whitehall. Consequently, references to the old bridge date the action of Dickens' novels in the past, before his writing career had begun; as in *Great Expectations*, 'It was old London bridge in those days' (*GE*, III, 7).

Dickens' first-hand knowledge of the bridge is apparent in his reference to its physical features, as when David sits in 'one of the stone recesses'. His detailed knowledge of London Bridge is all the more evident in *Oliver Twist*. In this novel, it features in another way characteristic of Dickens' use of bridges in his novels – as a meeting place. Nancy arranges to meet Rose Maylie and Mr Brownlow, in order to give them information that may help Oliver, but in doing so she puts her own life in danger. There is an elaborate interplay between the figures and the physical features of the bridge, as when Kaggs, Fagin's unidentified spy, shrinks into 'one of the recesses which surmount the piers of the bridge':

> The church clocks chimed three quarters past eleven as two figures emerged on London Bridge. One, which advanced with a swift and rapid step, was that of a woman, who looked eagerly about her as though in quest of some expected object; the other figure was that of a man, who slunk along in the deepest shadow he could find, and at some distance accommodated his pace to hers, stopping when she stopped, and, as she moved again, creeping stealthily on, but never allowing himself, in the ardour of his pursuit, to gain upon her footsteps. Thus they crossed the bridge from the Middlesex to the Surrey shore, when the woman, apparently disappointed in her anxious scrutiny of the foot-passengers, turned back. The movement was sudden, but he who watched her was not thrown off his guard by it, for shrinking into one of the recesses which surmount the piers of the bridge, and leaning over the parapet the better to conceal his figure,

he suffered her to pass by on the opposite pavement, and when she was about the same distance in advance as she had been before, he slipped quietly down and followed her again. At nearly the centre of the bridge she stopped. The man stopped too. (*OT,* 46)

After St Paul's strikes midnight, 'a young lady, accompanied by a grey-haired gentleman,' alights from a hackney carriage and head onto the bridge. Immediately Nancy moves towards them, but Kaggs, dressed 'in the garments of a countryman', brushes past them and alarms Nancy. In the subsequent exchange, Dickens demonstrates a detailed knowledge of the physical features of the bridge:

'Not here,' said Nancy hurriedly. 'I am afraid to speak to you here. Come away – out of the public road – down the steps yonder.'

As she uttered these words, and indicated with her hand the direction in which she wished them to proceed, the countryman looked round, and roughly asking what they took up the whole pavement for, passed on.

The steps to which the girl had pointed were those which, on the Surrey bank, and on the same side of the bridge as Saint Saviour's church, form a landing-stairs from the river. To this spot the man bearing the appearance of a countryman hastened unobserved; and after a moment's survey of the place, he began to descend.

These stairs are a part of the bridge; they consist of three flights.

Just below the end of the second, going down, the stone wall on the left terminates in an ornamental pilaster facing towards the Thames. At this point the lower steps widen, so that a person turning that angle of the wall is necessarily unseen by any others on the stairs who chance to be above him, if only a step. The countryman looked hastily round when he reached this point, and as there seemed no better place of concealment, and the tide being out there was plenty of room, he slipped aside, with his back to the pilaster, and there waited, pretty certain that they would come no lower, and that even if he could not hear what was said, he could follow them again with safety. (*OT*, 46)

When Nancy is left alone again, refusing Rose Maylie's offer of aid, she 'sunk down nearly at her full length upon one of the stone stairs, and vented the anguish of her heart in bitter tears'. The 1831 bridge has been replaced again since then, but the stone steps remain, integrated into the new bridge. A plaque on this spot commemorates its association with Dickens' novel. It mistakenly identifies the steps as the scene of Nancy's murder, rather than her betrayal of Sykes; it is only in the stage-musical adaptation of Dickens' novel that Nancy is murdered here.

SOUTHWARK BRIDGE

The first sentence of *Our Mutual Friend* (1865) notes that Gaffer and Lizzie Hexam drift their boat 'between Southwark Bridge which is of iron, and London Bridge which is of stone'. Southwark Bridge was opened in 1819 and was often commonly referred to as the 'Iron Bridge'.[2] It features extensively under that name in *Little Dorrit*, the novel that best reveals the imaginative resonances that bridges could have for Dickens.

The bridge was too narrow for most vehicles, so it was principally a pedestrian footbridge. It carried the least traffic of all the central London bridges due to the toll that was charged. Most people preferred the toll-free and flatter bridges – London and Blackfriars – on either side.[3] Its quietness is frequently mentioned in *Little Dorrit*, for that is why Amy Dorrit goes there so often. As with so many bridges for Dickens, this bridge provides the setting for quiet contemplation and for a significant meeting. Being the nearest alternative across the river to the busier London Bridge, the Iron Bridge witnesses a chance encounter between Arthur Clennam and Little Dorrit:

> The crowd in the street jostling the crowd in his mind, and the two crowds making a confusion, he avoided London Bridge, and turned off in the quieter direction of the Iron Bridge. He had scarcely set foot upon it, when he saw Little Dorrit walking on before him. It was a pleasant day, with a light breeze blowing, and she seemed to have that minute come there for air. He had left her in her father's room within an hour.
>
> It was a timely chance, favorable to his wish of observing her face and manner when no one else was by. He quickened his pace; but, before he reached her, she turned her head. (*LD*, I, 22)

The meeting and the ensuing conversation is memorable for both of them and the Iron Bridge becomes a quiet emblem of the connection between Amy and Arthur. When she tells him, much later in the novel, that it is good for her to stay with her father, Clennam responds, 'So you said that day, upon the bridge. I thought of it much afterwards.' When Little Dorrit writes to him from Venice about Henry Gowan's over-easy manner, she wonders how Clennam will receive the news: 'I wonder what you will say when you come to this! I know how you will look, and I can almost hear the voice in which you would tell me on the Iron Bridge.' This was not the first time they had been together here. In fact, the bridge already carried reminiscences of Arthur for Little Dorrit. It is likely that her pensive contemplations there are supposed at least partly to involve Arthur. It is probable that he is on her mind in this instance, as she readily recognises his approaching foot-step and she reacts with telling sensitivity to Clennam's kind words. On the first occasion, the quietness of the bridge was a reason for their choosing it:

> Clennam offered his arm to Little Dorrit, and Little Dorrit took it. 'Will you go by the Iron Bridge,' said he, 'where there is an escape from the noise of the street?' Little Dorrit answered, if he pleased…
>
> Thus they emerged upon the Iron Bridge, which was as quiet after the roaring streets, as though it had been open country. (*LD*, I, 9)

The associations of the Iron Bridge with the growing affection between Arthur and Amy are part of the secret language of the novel, the reticent manner in which it tells its love story. We suspect that John Chivery is doomed in his quest for Little Dorrit's love because he chooses to declare himself on the Iron Bridge. When Mr Dorrit tells Chivery that 'Amy has gone for an airing on the Iron Bridge. She has become quite partial to the Iron Bridge of late, and seems to like to walk there better than anywhere,' the association of the bridge with Clennam implies that John Chivery has a rival in Little Dorrit's affections:

> Little Dorrit's lover very soon laid down his penny on the toll-plate of the Iron Bridge, and came upon it looking about him for the well-known and well-beloved figure. At first he feared she was not there;

but as he walked on towards the Middlesex side, he saw her standing still, looking at the water. She was absorbed in thought, and he wondered what she might be thinking about. There were the piles of city roofs and chimneys, more free from smoke than on week-days; and there were the distant masts and steeples. Perhaps she was thinking about them. (*LD*, I, 18)

The lack of conviction here – 'the distant masts and steeples. Perhaps she was thinking about them' – indicates John Chivery's willing self-delusion. Given the personal resonances of the bridge in Little Dorrit's story, it is not likely that she is thinking about the buildings, nor about John Chivery.

THE THAMES

One reason that many Dickens characters take pause on London's bridges is that the bridges offer the best vantage points of the river that absorbs, focuses or stimulates their wandering thoughts. Clennam heads for Southwark Bridge, rather than London Bridge, when he feels 'the crowd in the street jostling the crowd in his mind'. For many of the characters on London's bridges, the setting and especially the river, offer an image of their inward thoughts or feelings.

For characters such as Nancy this can be ominous. When she meets Rose Maylie and Mr Brownlow on London Bridge, the river prompts a morbid fatalism. Rose wonders with deep concern about what sort of future lies in store for Nancy. Nancy replies:

'Look before you, lady. Look at that dark water. How many times do you read of such as we who spring into the tide, and leave no living thing to care for or bewail them. It may be years hence, or it may be only months, but I shall come to that at last.' (*OT*, 46)

Mrs Edson faces the same fate in Dickens' Christmas story, 'Mrs Lirriper's Lodgings'. Martha Endell contemplates it in *David Copperfield*. In 'Down with the Tide', an essay Dickens wrote for *Household Words*, we encounter a toll-taker at Waterloo Bridge who recounts stories of suicides he has witnessed. It was far from unheard of at the time. There were five hundred suicides in the Thames annually according to one estimate.[4] And the topic held a dark fascination for many Victorian writers and artists. The inevitability in Nancy's suggestion that a watery grave will necessarily be hers is also an idea that returns in Dickens' later uses of the river image, where its steady flow towards the sea itself becomes a symbol for the relentless onrushing of life towards a fixed destination.

Little Dorrit, by contrast, responds to the life and vitality of the river, as she looks at it from Southwark Bridge. She tells Clennam that she sometimes has a sensation that it was 'almost unfeeling' to walk there:

> 'To see the river, and so much sky, and so many objects, and such change and motion. Then to go back, you know, and find him in the same cramped place.' (*LD*, I, 22)

The associations of the river — with space and freedom of movement — bring to mind, by contrast, the confinement of her father in the Marshalsea debtors' prison.

The river stimulates different feelings for characters in other of Dickens' novels too. At dawn on the day of Pip's attempt to smuggle Magwitch away in a rowing boat, the river reveals to him and us his optimism. As the sun rises, 'a veil seemed to be drawn from the river, and millions of sparkles burst out upon its waters. From me too, a veil seemed to be drawn, and I felt strong and well' (*GE*, III, 14).

The river is used as a symbol most memorably — because most intensely — in *Dombey and Son*. As Paul Dombey Jr lies dying, the river is ominously suggestive to the ailing boy of his impending fate:

> His fancy had a strange tendency to wander to the river, which he knew was flowing through the great city; and now he thought how black it was, and how deep it would look, reflecting the hosts of stars — and more than all, how steadily it rolled away to meet the sea. (*DS*, 16)

As night comes, Paul is calm, but for one anxiety:

> His only trouble was, the swift and rapid river. He felt forced, sometimes, to try to stop it — to stem it with his childish hands — or choke its way with sand — and when he saw it coming on, resistless, he cried out! (*DS*, 16)

The river's relentless progress continues to trouble the boy: 'it is bearing me away, I think!' It does so up until his early death, when the novel reveals that the river had been speaking to him of his mortality and of the (resistless) approach of 'the distant shore', where his late mother awaits him.

As she recalls the light rippling like water on the walls of her brother's bedroom, Florence Dombey imagines the river less gloomily. She thinks that if she were unwell, her father's proud heart would be stirred, and she imagines him relenting towards her. Then we are told:

> The golden water she remembered on the wall, appeared to Florence, in the light of such reflections, only as a current flowing on to rest, and to a region where the dear ones, gone before, were waiting, hand in hand; and often when she looked upon the darker river rippling at her feet, she thought with awful wonder, but not terror, of that river which her brother had so often said was bearing him away. (*DS*, 24)

Florence's calm response of 'awful wonder' is different from the more troubled reaction of her brother to the river. What's more, the passage releases the silent pun that has lain beneath all Dickens' writing about the river. The 'reflections' are both those of the river, whether the light that is reflected in it or from it, and the contemplations of the characters that it evokes.

The same pun occurs in the other Dickens novel in which the Thames becomes a major motif, *Our Mutual Friend*. The Thames is as central to *Our Mutual Friend* as it is to London itself. As the river flows through the novel, it becomes a motif that unifies different and disparate aspects of this expansive fiction, to the extent that Algernon Swinburne could declare: 'the real protagonist ... is the river'.[5] Indeed, the river is a recurrent presence in the novel, and it takes on a symbolic, mythical, religious force in those episodes where John Harmon and Eugene Wrayburn are brought respectively out of the Thames, reborn to new life according to the traditional Christian imagery, and according to the futures that the novel has in store for them both. Immediately before Bradley Headstone viciously attacks him at the waterside, Eugene Wrayburn holds an inner dialogue with himself over whether or not to marry Lizzie and spare her reputation:

The rippling of the river seemed to cause a correspondent stir in his uneasy reflections. He would have laid them asleep if he could, but they were in movement, like the stream, and all tending one way with a strong current. As the ripple under the moon broke unexpectedly now and then, and palely flashed in a new shape and with a new sound, so parts of his thoughts started, unbidden, from the rest, and revealed their wickedness. (*OMF*, II, 4, 6)

The river becomes an image of Eugene's thoughts. Both stir and are rippled, both move strongly in a single direction, but are suddenly disturbed by opposite energies. The resourcefulness of the river, for Wrayburn, Amy Dorrit and countless other characters, is such that it not only awakens contemplation, but provides an image for those processes of the mind.

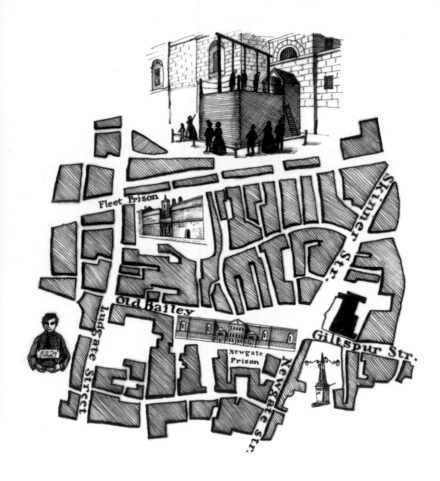

LONDON'S PRISONS

Throughout his fiction Dickens reflected on the feeling of being imprisoned. It was particularly his own experience as a writer, often confined in isolation in his own room. He soon started to hear an ominous pun in 'writer's pen'. Dickens' interest in prisons had its roots in personal experience – his father having been thrown into debtors' prison in 1824 – and it continued into adulthood as he wrote about prison reform and advocated humane prison conditions. His reactions to London's prisons are many and varied.[1] They result in mixed modes in his fictional presentation of the prisons, ranging from angry satire to gentle comedy, through grim realism and personal anxiety. His most powerful writing about prisons comes in those novels where the prison institution that is described comes to represent a way characters in and out of jail experience the confining nature of life in nineteenth-century London.

NEWGATE PRISON

One of the first prisons Dickens wrote about was Newgate Prison, in his sketch 'A Visit to Newgate' (1836).[2] There had long been a prison on the site, two hundred yards north-west of St Paul's, which is now occupied by part of the Old Bailey. The prison dated back to medieval London, when it was a gatehouse in the city wall. It was rebuilt several times including finally in 1770, although it had to be restored after the Gordon Riots of 1780. It was finally closed down in 1902 and its various parts, from the doors, to the bell, to leg chains and weights, were auctioned off.[3] Dickens had first visited the prison in 1835, prior to writing his sketch, and he returned on several subsequent occasions. Writing to round off the first volume of

Sketches by Boz, Dickens was especially interested in how he could convey the experience of being inside the prison within the confines of the written page. It was an interest that never left him, and he experiments with different styles and modes of writing about prisons throughout his long career.

In a sketch that inscribes an awareness of its own literary structures and procedures, Boz begins with the women's wing, replicating the chronology of his own visit: 'as we were introduced into this part of the building first, we will adopt the same order, and introduce our readers to it also'. But it is not always possible or practicable to replicate the structures of the prison within the structures of his prose. He has to omit any mention of intervening gates as he moves from ward to ward because 'if we noticed every gate that was unlocked for us to pass through and locked again as soon as we had passed, we should require a gate at every comma'.

One of the best effects of the first half of this sketch is the way that Dickens' writing reflects the involuted organisation of the prison. There are 'a number of tortuous and intricate windings, guarded in their turn by huge gates and gratings, whose appearance is sufficient to dispel at once the slightest hope of escape that any new comer may have entertained'. The prisoners therefore are constantly walking over the same ground, retracing their steps, pounding the same pavements. This is matched by a prose account that keeps being drawn back to the same locations:

> Leaving the chapel, descending to the passage so frequently alluded to, and crossing the yard before noticed as being allotted to prisoners of a more respectable description than the generality of men confined here, the visitor arrives at a thick iron gate of great size and strength. ('A Visit to Newgate', *SB*)

Just as Dickens retraces his steps in his visit, so his prose goes over old ground by referring back to places already mentioned, and drawing attention to the repetition.

Pip makes a visit to Newgate in *Great Expectations*. While waiting for Estella to arrive in London, he has some spare time on his hands and agrees to accompany Wemmick to the prison. Before revealing his destination, Wemmick asks Pip to guess where he is going:

> 'To the office?' said I, for he was tending in that direction.
>   'Next thing to it,' returned Wemmick, 'I am going to Newgate.' (*GE*, II, 13)

Jaggers' office, where Wemmick works, is next door to Newgate Prison, but there is a joke here that the office is the 'next thing' to the prison in more ways than one. Perhaps Wemmick knew what it was like to feel as though he were chained to his desk. Certainly, the constraining effect of life in the office was one aspect of Dickens' long held awareness that the capital's prisons loom large as metaphors for the experience of Londoners outside their walls.

I have said that Dickens' writing about prisons takes on different perspectives and in *Great Expectations*, Pip's visit to Newgate serves as a reminder of his own associations with crime and that sense of guilt that he carries with him throughout the novel, which now makes itself felt as a 'taint of prison and crime':

> I consumed the whole time in thinking how strange it was that I should be encompassed by all this taint of prison and crime; that, in my childhood out on our lonely marshes on a winter evening I should have first encountered it; that, it should have reappeared on two occasions, starting out like a stain that was faded but not gone; that, it should in this new way pervade my fortune and advancement. While my mind was thus engaged, I thought of the beautiful young Estella, proud and refined, coming towards me, and I thought with absolute abhorrence of the contrast between the jail and her. I wished that Wemmick had not met me, or that I had not yielded to him and gone with him, so that, of all days in the year on this day, I might not have had Newgate in my breath and on my clothes. I beat the prison dust off my feet as I sauntered to and fro, and I shook it out of my dress, and I exhaled its air from my lungs. So contaminated did I feel, remembering who was coming, that the coach came quickly after all, and I was not yet free from the soiling consciousness of Mr. Wemmick's conservatory, when I saw her face at the coach window and her hand waving to me. (*GE*, II, 13)

FLEET PRISON

The Fleet, too, is one of London's historic prisons. Dating back to the twelfth century, it was the first prison in London to be conceived, designed and built as a jail. Originally standing on the east bank of the River Fleet, Dickens would have known it after the river had been driven underground. The site now is on the eastern side of Farringdon Street, about halfway between Ludgate Circus and the bridge of the Holborn Viaduct.[4] The Fleet features in Dickens' first novel. Mr Pickwick is incarcerated there for refusing to pay 'damages and costs' after the court finds for the prosecution in the breach of promise action taken against him by Mrs Bardell:

> The usual forms having been gone through, the body of Samuel Pickwick was soon afterwards confided to the custody of the tip-staff, to be by him taken to the Warden of the Fleet Prison, and there detained until the amount of the damages and costs in the action of Bardell against Pickwick was fully paid and satisfied.
>
> 'And that,' said Mr Pickwick laughing, 'will be a very long time. Sam, call another hackney coach. Perker, my dear friend, good bye.' (*PP*, 40)

Mr Pickwick's defiance is matched only by his complete disregard for the shame and punishment supposedly heaped upon him by his incarceration. In fact, such is his magnificent indifference, that he thinks of the prison welcoming him, as if he were merely putting up at a hotel. When he arrives in the interior of the prison, he is told he will have to stay there 'until he had undergone the ceremony, known to the initiated, as "sitting for your portrait"'. This feeds Pickwick's belief in the importance of his arrival and the hospitality he is likely to meet:

> 'Sitting for my portrait!' said Mr Pickwick.
>
> 'Having your likeness taken, Sir,' replied the stout turnkey. 'We're capital hands at likenesses here. Take 'em in no time, and always exact. Walk in, Sir, and make yourself at home.'
>
> Mr Pickwick complied with the invitation, and sat himself down, when Mr Weller, who stationed himself at the back of the chair,

whispered that the sitting was merely another term for undergoing an inspection by the different turnkeys, in order that they might know prisoners from visitors.

'Well, Sam,' said Mr Pickwick, 'then I wish the artists would come. This is rather a public place.' (*PP*, 40)

Mr Pickwick's casual indifference to being locked up in jail sets the tone for those later characters who are equally able to make themselves 'at home' in debtors' prison, Mr Micawber and Mr Dorrit. It seems to become a way for Dickens to inoculate himself from the shame of the prison that had intruded into his own life by imagining characters who were serenely unconcerned by it.

The Fleet was closed in 1842, when the laws on debt were changed, and it was razed a few years later. Mr Pickwick's apathy notwithstanding, Dickens still sounded a note of triumph, in his 1867 preface to the novel, when he observed that 'legal reforms have pared the claws of Messrs. Dodson and Fogg; ... the laws relating to imprisonment for debt are altered; and the Fleet prison is pulled down!' The novel's comic spirit had not distracted Dickens from his own serious-minded derision of the injustices of the prison system and of the Fleet itself.

KING'S BENCH PRISON

There are similar strands of indignation and comic relish in Dickens' writing about the King's Bench prison – another of London's ancient prisons, used, in Dickens' day, to house debtors. It stood near the Marshalsea in Southwark, at the eastern end of Borough Road, near the High Street, where it had been rebuilt from 1755. As recorded in *Barnaby Rudge* (1841), it was set mightily on fire during the Gordon Riots. It was rebuilt there-after, and finally pulled down in 1880.

In *Nicholas Nickleby*, Dickens' satiric ire is directed against the legislation that meant that those thrown into debtors' prison who had or could obtain some money, could use it to take lodgings within the vicinity of the prison, known as a 'liberty', or the 'Rules', rather than to pay their creditors:

The place to which Mr. Cheeryble had directed him was a row of mean and not over-cleanly houses, situated within 'the Rules' of the King's Bench Prison, and not many hundred paces distant from the obelisk in Saint George's Fields. The Rules are a certain liberty adjoining the prison, and comprising some dozen streets in which debtors who can raise money to pay large fees, from which their creditors do *not* derive any benefit, are permitted to reside by the wise provisions of the same enlightened laws which leave the debtor who can raise no money to starve in jail, without the food, clothing, lodging, or warmth, which are provided for felons convicted of the most atrocious crimes that can disgrace humanity. There are many pleasant fictions of the law in constant operation, but there is not one so pleasant or practically humorous as that which supposes every man to be of equal value in its impartial eye, and the benefits of all laws to be equally attainable by all men, without the smallest reference to the furniture of their pockets. (*NN*, 46)

But when Mr Micawber takes up his abode there early in *David Copperfield*, Dickens' writing about the prison avoids his earlier disgruntlement at the injustices of prison legislation and is more concerned with the personal response to the situation of Mr Micawber, David and Mrs Micawber. The prisoner himself bears up well:

> At last Mr. Micawber's difficulties came to a crisis, and he was arrested early one morning, and carried over to the King's Bench Prison in the Borough. He told me, as he went out of the house, that the God of day had now gone down upon him – and I really thought his heart was broken and mine too. But I heard, afterwards, that he was seen to play a lively game at skittles, before noon. (*DC*, 11)

David's reaction to the King's Bench Prison is more miserable and more pained. Like those several characters in Dickens who, once acquainted with the prison, feel themselves carrying the 'prison taint' away with them, when David moves to Dr Strong's school, he cannot rid himself of the shame of the association and the fear that the other boys might find it out:

> My mind ran upon what they would think, if they knew of my familiar acquaintance with the King's Bench Prison? Was there anything about me which would reveal my proceedings in connexion with the Micawber family – all those pawnings, and sellings, and suppers – in spite of myself? Suppose some of the boys had seen me coming through Canterbury, wayworn and ragged, and should find me out? What would they say, who made so light of money, if they could know how I had scraped my halfpence together, for the purchase of my daily saveloy and beer, or my slices of pudding? How would it affect them, who were so innocent of London life, and London streets, to discover how knowing I was (and was ashamed to be) in some of the meanest phases of both? All this ran in my head so much,

on that first day at Doctor Strong's, that I felt distrustful of my slightest look and gesture; shrunk within myself whensoever I was
approached by one of my new schoolfellows; and hurried off the
minute school was over, afraid of committing myself in my response
to any friendly notice or advance. (*DC*, 16)

Dickens' various responses to the King's Bench Prison, then,
range between the social indignation of *Nicholas Nickleby* and the
personal shame of *David Copperfield*. Micawber's fond imagining
of the prison as a happy community, which anticipates Mr Dorrit,
is in some ways an attractive response, as it is immune to the
pricks of embarrassment and shame. Perhaps these characters'
willing indifference to the prison is a self-protective way of
responding to, or defeating, the shame, but one that Dickens
must have thought himself too sensitive and sensible to maintain.

PENTONVILLE

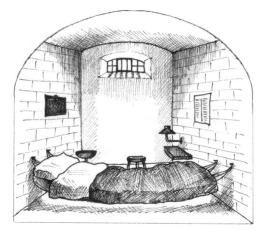

Pentonville Prison, opened in 1842, was one of London's first
modern prisons. It remains in operation today on its original
site on the Caledonian Road in north London. It was built
with five wings radiating from a central hall, an architecture

suitable for the 'separate system' of solitary confinement. Pentonville was referred to as the Model Prison because it was deemed to be exemplary in its arrangements and because it became the model for scores of other prisons built across the British Empire throughout the 1840s.

The prison had been expensive to build and it was expensive to run. The prisoners were well looked after and well fed, even if they were in apparent isolation. Dickens was disturbed by the contrast it created between the conditions of the inmates and those of paupers and even country labourers, who were not able to live by their own honest means at equivalent comfort[5].

He wrote an article in *Household Words* in 1850 which laid out the arguments against the 'separate system'. The article, called 'Pet Prisoners', has a productively uneven tone of voice. At the outset, it is a sober-minded piece, judiciously setting forward arguments against the system of solitary confinement at the Model Prison. In places it sounds quaintly Victorian, with its stiff-lipped editorial 'we' and a cautiously rational articulation of its claims: 'We shall consider it, first in the relation of the extraordinary contrast it presents … We shall then inquire, and endeavour to lay before our readers some means of judging …', etc.

Dickens strives to keep his satirical edge blunted, but in the early paragraphs it occasionally glimmers through the guarded prose:

> This Model Prison had cost at the close of 1847, under the heads of 'building' and 'repairs' alone, the insignificant sum of ninety-three thousand pounds – within seven thousand pounds of the amount of the last government grant for the Education of the whole people, and enough to pay for the emigration to Australia of four thousand, six hundred and fifty poor persons at twenty pounds per head. ('Pet Prisoners', *SJ*)

The spelling out of the numbers suggests a mathematical precision to the case against the prison, but the description of the vast expenditure as 'the insignificant sum' is a barbed adjective that punctures the solemnly factual tone. Even the frequent references to the 'Model' prison in this critical account can come to seem facetious under the pressure of repetition.

There are early and late examples in the essay of a building rhetoric, indicative of the strength of Dickens' feeling on the subject, and this has more of an outlet later in the piece, as it becomes more conversational in style, more imaginative and more playful. The playfulness is apparent when Dickens observes that the one argument usually put forward most determinedly in favour of keeping prisoners separate from each other is that they should not have to be identifiable to their former prisoners once they have been released. He judges that 'Nor have we any sufficient guarantee that even this solitary point is gained.' He might have written it with a glint in his eye, as he knows that there are two senses in which 'this solitary point' can be understood.

The essay becomes wittier and more imaginative once Dickens relays, with stifled relish, the intrigues and conspiracies of the prisoners to break the ban on communication. It really comes to life when he starts to imagine the thoughts of the inmates and to inhabit their voices (which he does for the imagined prisoner, 'John Styles'). In the second half of the essay, Dickens' attention is drawn to those aspects of the 'separate system' that make for intriguing stories:

> Under how many apparently insuperable difficulties, men immured in solitary cells, will by some means obtain a knowledge of other men immured in other solitary cells, most of us know from all the accounts and anecdotes we have read of secret prisons and secret prisoners from our school-time upwards. ('Pet Prisoners', *SJ*)

Dickens recognises the fictional potential of Pentonville's 'secret' system. These possibilities are worked out in *David Copperfield*, in the late chapter where Dickens satirises the 'separate system' of Pentonville Prison. David and Traddles visit a Model Prison, where they are shocked to find Uriah Heep and Littimer – two 'interesting penitents' – being lauded as model prisoners, deeply regretful of their wrongdoing and imploring all others to avoid the same pitfalls, embodying, of course, the 'pattern penitence' that Dickens had lampooned in 'Pet Prisoners'. Released from the essay form and its predisposition towards structured, logical argument, Dickens develops a memorably imaginative satire as part of his novel. The narrative potential that Dickens discerned in the 'secret system' is realised here, as he creates a sort of 'recognition scene' within the chapter. Prisoner Number Twenty-Seven is discussed, but we do not know until he arrives that it is Uriah Heep. The surprise of his appearance is part of the effect of the chapter, and it relies for its effect on the prison operating according to the model of the solitary system.

Dickens the essayist had deplored the injustice of the contrast between the conditions of those inside and those outside:

> In the prison, every man receives five pints and a quarter of liquid cocoa weekly (made of flaked cocoa or cocoa-nibs,) with fourteen ounces of milk and forty-two drams of molasses; also seven pints of gruel weekly, sweetened with forty-two drams of molasses. In the workhouse, every able-bodied adult receives fourteen pints and a half of milk-porridge weekly, and no cocoa, and no gruel. ('Pet Prisoners', SJ)

Dickens the novelist satirises the relative nicety of supplying cocoa to the prisoners through one of the patron's exchanges with Littimer, prisoner Twenty-Eight:

> 'Twenty Eight,' said a gentleman in spectacles, who had not yet spoken, 'you complained last week, my good fellow, of the cocoa. How has it been since?'
> 'I thank you, sir,' said Mr. Littimer, 'it has been better made. If I might take the liberty of saying so, sir, I don't think the milk which is boiled with it is quite genuine; but I am aware, sir, that there is great adulteration of milk, in London, and that the article in a pure state is difficult to be obtained.' (DC, 61)

By this stage in the novel, David has established himself as a writer of much success. Like Dickens, David found in London life a creative spur: 'Occasionally, I went to London; to lose myself in the swarm of life there' (DC, 61). It seems that this visit to the Model Prison was made available to him because he was a writer, which is also why the prisons were opened up to Dickens. For Dickens, the experiment at Pentonville Prison aroused indignation and social concern, but his most memorable written response was satirical.

MARSHALSEA

It is in *Little Dorrit* that Dickens' writing about prisons famously reached its apogee. Mr Dorrit is locked up in the Marshalsea – the same prison of which John Dickens had been an inmate in 1824. Anticipating his parallel comments in 1867 about the

Fleet Prison, Dickens remarks in the opening description of the Marshalsea that the jail has now been demolished:

> Thirty years ago there stood, a few doors short of the church of Saint George, in the Borough of Southwark, on the left hand side of the way going southward, the Marshalsea Prison. It had stood there many years before, and it remained there some years afterwards; but it is gone now, and the world is none the worse without it. (*LD*, I, 6)

The Marshalsea dated back to the fourteenth century. Like the Fleet, it was closed down in 1842, more than a decade before Dickens began the novel that would immortalise it. In 1857, he went to see what remained of the prison. He reported his findings in a subsequent preface:

> Some of my readers may have an interest in being informed whether or no any portions of the Marshalsea Prison are yet standing. I did not know, myself, until the sixth of this present month, when I went to look. I found the outer front courtyard, often mentioned here, metamorphosed into a butter shop; and I then almost gave up every brick of the jail for lost. Wandering, however, down a certain adjacent 'Angel Court, leading to Bermondsey', I came to 'Marshalsea Place:' the houses in which I recognised, not only as the great block of the former prison, but as preserving the rooms that arose in my mind's-eye when I became Little Dorrit's biographer. (*LD*, Preface)

Little of what Dickens saw remains now. But in an alleyway named Angel Place, on one side of St George's Gardens, part of the old Marshalsea's south wall is still standing.

Dickens continues his opening description of the Marshalsea with an account of the ramshackle houses that were walled off to form the prison:

> It was an oblong pile of barrack building, partitioned into squalid houses standing back to back, so that there were no back rooms; environed by a narrow paved yard, hemmed in by high walls duly spiked at top. Itself a close and confined prison for debtors, it contained within it a much closer and more confined jail for smugglers. Offenders against the revenue laws, and defaulters to excise or customs, who had incurred fines which they were unable to pay, were supposed to be incarcerated behind an iron-plated door, closing up a second prison, consisting of a strong cell or two, and a blind alley some yard and a half wide, which formed the mysterious termination of the very limited skittle-ground in which the Marshalsea debtors bowled down their troubles.
>
> Supposed to be incarcerated there, because the time had rather outgrown the strong cells and the blind alley. In practice they had come to be considered a little too bad, though in theory they were quite as good as ever; which may be observed to be the case at the

present day with other cells that are not at all strong, and with other
blind alleys that are stone-blind. Hence the smugglers habitually
consorted with the debtors (who received them with open arms),
except at certain constitutional moments when somebody came from
some Office, to go through some form of overlooking something,
which neither he nor anybody else knew anything about. On those
truly British occasions, the smugglers, if any, made a feint of walking
into the strong cells and the blind alley, while this somebody pretended
to do his something; and made a reality of walking out again as soon as
he hadn't done it – neatly epitomising the administration of most of
the public affairs in our right little, tight little, island. (*LD*, I, 6)

Dickens' bridling at the inhumanity of many forms of imprisonment is apparent here, but his criticism of those public offi-
cials who monitor the prison is not as sharp as the pointed
criticisms of *Nicholas Nickleby* had been. He is not criticising a
particular aspect of prison legislation so much as finding in the
prisons and their officers an 'epitome' of most of Britain's
public affairs. The grim, factual description of the prison is
already turning, here on its first appearance, into a metaphor of
British life in the nineteenth century.

This is the novel in which Dickens invents – and lacerates –
the Circumlocution Office, the government department that
specialises in 'How Not to Do It'. Its function in the novel is to
stifle the aspirations of characters such as Doyce and Clennam,
limiting, constricting, confining their hopes and opportunities,
in a way that makes the prison seem to be a metaphor for life in
London at the time, as Dickens saw it.

Certainly, the prison exerts an effect beyond its own walls in the
novel. Little Dorrit confesses to Arthur Clennam, at one stage, that
'It was but the other day that my sister told me I had become so
used to the prison that I had its tone and character.' And the
Marshalsea repeatedly has that effect on characters. It so tarnishes
them with a prison taint that they are constrained by the prison
even outside its walls. That sense of constraint is so recurrent in
the novel, that the novel too, and its plot, has the 'tone and
character' of the Marshalsea. Little Dorrit's dissolute brother,
Tip, is one character who carries the prison taint with him:

> But whatever Tip went into, he came out of tired, announcing that he
> had cut it. Wherever he went, this foredoomed Tip appeared to take the
> prison walls with him, and to set them up in such trade or calling; and
> to prowl about within their narrow limits in the old slip-shod, purpose-
> less, down-at-heel way; until the real immoveable Marshalsea walls
> asserted their fascination over him, and brought him back. (*LD*, I, 7)

The prison's sense of containment is therefore transferred beyond
its own high walls and into the rest of the novel. Sometimes this
is explicitly the case. Pondering a possible link between Mr
Dorrit's incarceration and his mother's confinement in her
wheelchair and her room, Arthur Clennam imagines her saying:
'He withers away in his prison; I wither away in mine; inexorable
justice is done; what do I owe on this score!' The symmetry
between these two imprisonments – literal and metaphorical – is
expressly articulated in the novel and by Mrs Clennam in
particular, but it comes to signify, even more deeply, that there is a
causal relationship between the two cases, as we discover that
Mrs Clennam is guilty of betraying Little Dorrit of her rightful
riches. Her word 'inexorable' is a yet more subtle indication of
the pervasive presence of the Marshalsea as a massive metaphor
in the novel, both because it constantly pulls people back to itself,
but also because the novel's interest in fatedness itself seems to be
a product of the prison within its pages.

LONDON'S CHURCHES

Wherever you turn in Dickens' London, you see a church. They are a keynote of his fiction. He was responding to the reality of the city, because churches were ubiquitous in nineteenth-century London. The number of buildings has long outstripped demand, especially in the City, which has never been a major residential area since the Great Fire. And yet there were nearly one hundred churches within the City at the time. The fire burnt eighty-seven of them and fifty-one were rebuilt by Sir Christopher Wren over the subsequent thirty years.[1] During the nineteenth century, several of Wren's city churches were destroyed.[2] A great many new churches were built, located more widely across the metropolis, as part of new initiatives to cater for the growing population, including the rebuilding of St Dunstan's in the West.[3] London's churches are locations for christenings, weddings and funerals in Dickens' writing – major events and milestones in most of his work. Westminster Abbey and St Paul's Cathedral also frequently feature as part of the cityscape. Dickens' attention is often drawn to the clocks of various churches, which prompt narrative reflections on the passing of time, or, in strangely Dickensian ways, ideas about the distortion of time, which seem to be emblems of the temporal distortions that the novels put into play. He frequently notices in his writing the church bells, which ring out to summon people to church or to mark the passing hours.[4]

According to an *Uncommercial Traveller* paper, 'City of London Churches', Dickens spent much of 1860 visiting the many old churches in the heart of London:

> On summer Sundays, in the gentle rain or the bright sunshine either, deepening the idleness of the idle City I have sat, in that singular silence which belongs to resting-places usually astir, in scores of buildings at the

heart of the world's metropolis, unknown to far greater numbers of
people speaking the English tongue, than the ancient edifices of the
Eternal City, or the Pyramids of Egypt. The dark vestries and registries
into which I have peeped, and the little hemmed-in churchyards that
have echoed to my feet, have left impressions on my memory as distinct
and quaint as any it has in that way received. In all those dusty registers
that the worms are eating, there is not a line but made some hearts leap,
or some tears flow, in their day. Still and dry now, still and dry! and the old
tree at the window with no room for its branches, has seen them all out.
So with the tomb of the old Master of the old Company, on which it
drips. His son restored it and died, his daughter restored it and died, and
then he had been remembered long enough, and the tree took possession
of him, and his name cracked out. ('City of London Churches', *UT*)[5]

The deserted ancient churches give rise to the sense that the
life of the City vastly exceeds individual human lives. City
Time outlasts individual human time. The effects can be
humbling and attention is drawn to those old worthies whose
names are no longer remembered, literally 'cracked out' by
the tree in the graveyard. Throughout Dickens' fiction,
churches summon up these long perspectives of time, in
which humanity feels its insignificance. Frequently, London's
churches, the bells that chime out, or the dome of St Paul's
that appears atop the cityscape, draw characters or the narrative voice itself into a pseudo-spiritual, quasi-theological
reflection on their situations.

ST DUNSTAN'S IN THE WEST

It may be that Dickens had St Dustan's in the West in mind
when he wrote his second Christmas book, *The Chimes* (1844).
The church still stands in Fleet Street. It is one of the oldest
churches in central London, founded around the time of the
Norman Conquest. Little of the ancient church remains today
– the present building was erected in 1832 and the tower was
rebuilt after bombing destroyed it in the Second World War.
The church is not named in the tale, but Clarkson Stanfield

depicts it, with the distinctive octagonal lantern at the top of the square tower, in one of the illustrations. Dickens' description of the church latches immediately onto its ancient history.

> High up in the steeple of an old church, far above the light and murmur of the town and far below the flying clouds that shadow it, is the wild and dreary place at night: and high up in the steeple of an old church, dwelt the Chimes I tell of.

> They were old Chimes, trust me. Centuries ago, these bells had
> been baptized by bishops: so many centuries ago, that the register of
> their baptism was lost long, long before the memory of man, and no
> one knew their names. (*The Chimes*, CB)

If the ancient churches of London are associated in Dickens'
mind with the long sweep of historical time, then St Dunstan's
is no exception. But the church reflects another habit of
Dickens' writing, the surprising presence of that which is
grotesque, or imaginative, or fanciful in the heart of the city.
Dickens was frequently drawn to its remarkable and distinctive
clock, still prominent on the facade of the church today. The
clock dates back to the seventeenth century and was the first
public clock in London to have a minute hand. But its attraction
for Dickens – and for David Copperfield – was the two figures,
possibly Gog and Magog, who strike the bells with their clubs.
Accompanied by his aunt, David stops at St Dunstan's with the
express intention of catching sight of the two figures:

> We made a pause at the toy-shop in Fleet-street, to see the giants of
> Saint Dunstan's strike upon the bells – we had timed our going, so as
> to catch them at it, at twelve o'clock – and then went on towards
> Ludgate Hill, and St Paul's Churchyard. (*DC*, 23)

In 'Gone Astray', the wonderful account of Dickens as a boy
lost in London, he again pauses in front of the church:

> I came... on the figures at St Dunstan's! Who could see those obliging
> monsters strike upon the bells and go? ('Gone Astray', *SJ*)

'Obliging monsters' is a good way to describe these two fantastical
creatures that are marshalled entirely by the ticking of the
clock, serving a useful function with a regularity entirely at
odds with their supposed nature. While Dickens expresses the
impossibility of ignoring these captivating creatures, he also
provides us with the rewards of keen observation in his
description of them. It shows the child–observer relaying things
as he sees them, repeating not resolving the inconsistencies: the

'obliging' and the monstrous. As has been shown many times, the perspective of the child is central to Dickens' imaginative vision, and the childlike fear and pleasure of the monstrous, combined with the adult's enjoyment of the orderly, are characteristic twin impulses throughout Dickens' writing. His writing about London is no exception to this as he relishes the sprawling, unpredictable nature of the city, but also seeks to contain it in his prose, and to admire legislation that regulates it or transport networks that organise it. He finds in its churches points of constancy amid the chaos, points of stability from which he can survey the city at large.

ST GEORGE'S

The church involved in the action of *Little Dorrit* itself provides an ordering function in that novel. Early in the novel, we learn that Little Dorrit was christened at the church of St George the Martyr, Southwark, with the prison turnkey as her impromptu godfather: 'the turnkey went up to the font of Saint George's church, and promised and vowed and renounced on her behalf, as he himself related when he came back, 'like a good 'un'' (*LD*, 7).

The Marshalsea prison is 'a few doors short of the church of Saint George', making it the church nearest to the action in *Little Dorrit*. It still stands in its old location, on the busy Borough High Street in Southwark. Part of the wall of the old Marshalsea, already demolished when Dickens began writing his novel, remains along the north side of the churchyard. In the nineteenth century, prisoners who died in the Marshalsea, and at the nearby King's Bench Prison, were often taken to St George's to be buried. In the well-known chapter, 'Little Dorrit's party', Little Dorrit returns to the church with Maggy to catch an hour's sleep before dawn, after they have spent the night shut out from the Marshalsea. The kind-hearted verger welcomes her in, delighted to meet one of the church's 'curiosities', by which term he refers to her unique status as 'child of

the Marshalsea', born in the prison and never absent from it for so much as a day or night, until this night. He first shows her her name in the register of births, before giving her the burial register as a pillow:

> He was a very good old fellow, in his familiar way; and having stirred the Vestry fire, he looked round the shelves of registers for a particular volume. 'Here you are, you see,' he said, taking it down and turning the leaves. 'Here you'll find yourself, as large as life. Amy, daughter of William and Fanny Dorrit. Born, Marshalsea Prison, Parish of Saint George. And we tell people that you have lived there, without so much as a day's or a night's absence, ever since. Is it true?' […]
>
>   'Stop a bit. I must put something under the cushion for your head. Here's a Burial volume. Just the thing! We have got Mrs Bangham in this book. But what makes these books interesting to most people is

– not who's in 'em, but who isn't – who's coming, you know, and when. That's the interesting question.'

Commendingly looking back at the pillow he had improvised, he left them to their hour's repose. Maggy was snoring already, and Little Dorrit was soon fast asleep, with her head resting on that sealed book of Fate, untroubled by its mysterious blank leaves. (*LD,* I, 14)

The three volumes of births, marriages and deaths indicate the role that the church plays at key stages in the lives of many of its parishioners. Their involvement in Little Dorrit's story reminds the reader that she has a past and a future as well as a present, and marks out the phases of her life memorably. It heightens the significance of the occasion when she is shut out from the Marshalsea, by linking it to her birth and christening, and to the possibilities of her future fate, marriage and later death, though she is unheeding of this eventual future at this stage.

Finally, she is welcomed back to the church on her wedding day at the close of the novel:

Then they went up the steps of the neighbouring St George's Church, and went up to the altar, where Daniel Doyce was waiting in his paternal character. And there, was Little Dorrit's old friend who had given her the Burial Register for a pillow: full of admiration that she should come back to them to be married, after all.

And they were married, with the sun shining on them through the painted figure of Our Saviour on the window. And they went into the very room where Little Dorrit had slumbered after her party, to sign the Marriage Register. (*LD,* II, 34)

The image of the rays of light shining on them through the stained glass window is one by which Dickens applies a faint Christian sheen to the episode, typical of the gentle brand of broad Christianity suggested by his novels.

The novel, and the verger, summarise Little Dorrit's continued association with the church:

Little Dorrit's old friend held the inkstand as she signed her name, and the clerk paused in taking off the good clergyman's surplice, and all the witnesses looked on with special interest. 'For, you see,' said

Little Dorrit's old friend, 'this young lady is one of our curiosities, and has come now to the third volume of our Registers. Her birth is in what I call the first volume; she lay asleep on this very floor, with her pretty head on what I call the second volume; and she's now a-writing her little name as a bride, in what I call the third volume.' (*LD*, II, 34)

The presence of the church in the novel turns its events into narrative. It reminds us at key stages in Little Dorrit's life that she has a story that extends beyond the present moment. In a novel fascinated by memory and anticipation, the references to the volumes of church registers prompt us to think of Little Dorrit's history and her possible future. St George's church is a place of return for Little Dorrit, as if measuring out the periods of her life with the same regularity as the chiming of its bells or the beating of its clock.

ST PAUL'S

It is St Paul's Cathedral that most frequently in Dickens' work awakens thoughts of the larger significance of characters' lives, whether from secular or religious perspectives. As its dome appears on the city's horizon, Dickens encourages thoughts about the long spans of time that its presence suggests and that put into perspective the brevity of human concerns. The origins of the Cathedral are thought to date back to as early as AD 604, when a timber structure was first erected on the present site. It is located in the heart of the City of London, now with pedestrian access across the river by the Millennium Bridge, but its dome is readily visible from Blackfriars, Southwark and London bridges nearby. As it rises above the city as a whole, it reminds Dickens of the inequalities that exist within its shadow, as it were, and of the vanity of self-occupied pride.

When David Copperfield returns from his sojourn on the continent, he 'half expected to find St Paul's Cathedral looking older' (*DC*, 59), an absurd speculation that takes the famous

Cathedral to be a model of constancy, whilst also rendering it subject to the feelings of those who look upon it. Jo, the crossing-sweep in *Bleak House*, looks at the lofty dome from down by Blackfriars Bridge:

> And there he sits, munching and gnawing, and looking up at the great Cross on the summit of St Paul's Cathedral, glittering above a red and violet-tinted cloud of smoke. From the boy's face one might suppose that sacred emblem to be, in his eyes, the crowning confusion of the great, confused city; so golden, so high up, so far out of his reach. (*BH*, 19)

Dickens supposes that the cross on the dome of St Paul's might alert Jo to the inequalities in the city that are at odds with the just, loving, compassionate ethos of the Christian religion for which it is a symbol. The simplicity of the vision at the end of this chapter carries added weight because it follows directly from the harsh and hypocritical preaching of the Reverend Chadband, who condemns Jo's lack of spiritual understanding, whilst leaving him to starve.

St Paul's Cathedral is an ever-present reminder in Dickens' work of the perspectives of equality, mortality and human insignificance, in which his fiction often situates the actions of his characters. This is most directly apparent in an early chapter of *Master Humphrey's Clock* (1840-1), where Dickens considers the building of the cathedral's dome:

As I looked afar up into the lofty dome, I could not help wondering what were his reflections whose genius reared that mighty pile, when, the last small wedge of timber fixed, the last nail driven into its home for many centuries, the clang of hammers and the hum of busy voices gone, and the great silence whole years of noise had helped to make, reigning undisturbed around, he mused, as I did now, upon his work, and lost himself amid its vast extent. I could not quite determine whether the contemplation of it would impress him with a sense of greatness or of insignificance; but when I remembered how long a time it had taken to erect, in how short a space it might be traversed even to its remotest parts, for how brief a term he, or any of those who cared to bear his name, would live to see it, or know of its existence, I imagined him far more melancholy than proud, and looking with regret upon his labour done. (*MHC*, 6)[6]

Dickens imagines the dome prompting in the builder melancholy feelings of the brevity and ultimate insignificance of his own life, to a large degree because those were the associations it had for Dickens too.

The language and the cadence of the passage have a biblical ring, as does its moral vision. The internal drama of psychology ('As I looked … I could not help wondering … but when I remembered …') is reminiscent of the voice of the Preacher in the book of Ecclesiastes, with its large moral vision of the vanity of human labour; for example: 'Then I looked on all the works that my hands had wrought, and on the labour that I had laboured to do: and, behold, all was vanity and vexation of spirit, and there was no profit under the sun' (Ecclesiastes 2.11). It is part of the novelist's ability to rise out of the particulars of a fiction to larger, moral perspectives, and the distant presence of the dome of St Paul's constantly invokes those longer perspectives in Dickens' writing.

The rhythm of the passage frequently settles into the same rhythms as the hymns that, to this day, reverberate around the lofty dome of St Paul's. In fact, with remarkable compulsion the passage tends towards iambic tetrameter, or Common Metre, the traditional metrical pattern of English hymns, in which a short stress is followed by a long, four times over (Ama / zing Grace, / how sweet / the sound). This is most evident in the sentences with a suspended verb, which gives them an archaic, hymn-like structure: 'the last small wedge of timber fixed', 'the hum of busy voices gone' and 'regret upon his labour done'; but it is apparent with regularity throughout the paragraph: 'whose genius reared the mighty pile', 'whole years of noise had helped to make', and 'himself amid its vast extent'. As the passage tends towards this regular cadence, it is as if it is striving to reach a composed religious and philosophical perspective that calms the breathless, hectic rhythms of everyday life in London.

These regular rhythms are also instilled in Dickens' mind by the ticking of the Cathedral's great clock. His narrator pauses to reflect on the clock at the top of the church:

> I sat down opposite it, and hearing its regular and never-changing voice, that one deep constant note, uppermost amongst all the noise and clatter in the streets below – marking that, let that tumult rise or fall, go on or stop – let it be night or noon, tomorrow or today, this

> year or next – it still performed its functions with the same dull
> constancy, and regulated the progress of life around, the fancy came
> upon me that this was London's heart, and that when it should cease
> to beat, the city would be no more. (*MHC,* 6)

There is an admirable constancy to the beating of the clock,
which reflects the tranquil, well-regulated mind that is not
buffeted by fame and fortune, by time and chance. Yet Dickens'
description is double edged. The 'dull constancy' of the clock
anticipates the 'dull monotony' of the church bells that Clennam
hears on a dismal Sunday in *Little Dorrit*, and sounds less than
enthusiastic. The apocalyptic vision, of when 'the city would be
no more', offers the advantages of a religiously lengthened
perspective, but itself constitutes a melancholy prospect. The
abstract vision encouraged by Dickens' narrative voice on occasions never entirely drowns out the messy, irregular heartbeat of
his work. It does his characters good to reflect on the humbling
brevity of their lives and on the knowledge that the world will
go on without them, but Dickens knows too that life and his
own fiction comes, primarily, from the press and throng of the
London streets.

Given the profound associations of St Paul's in his eyes,
Dickens took a dim view of the cheapening exercise of
charging for admission. Almost in passing at the outset of the
sketch, he notes that 'I paid my fee of twopence, upon entering,
to one of the money-changers who sit within the Temple', but
the quick allusion is damning, as it compares the fee-collectors
to the 'money-changers', whose tables Jesus angrily overturned
in the Jerusalem Temple.

WESTMINSTER ABBEY

The practice of charging for admission was common at one of
London's other great churches, Westminster Abbey. Dickens
criticised it for this in a chapter of *Pictures from Italy*, where he

was impressed by an official at a cemetery in Bologna, who efficiently and interestingly described the monuments to his visitors for no charge: (*MHC*, 6)

> They would no more have such a man for a Verger in Westminster Abbey, than they would let the people in (as they do at Bologna) to see the monuments for nothing. (*PI*, 6)

The charge was gradually reduced, until it was eradicated altogether, and Dickens added a note to the published volume of *Pictures from Italy* (1846) to the effect that: 'A far more liberal and just recognition of the public has arisen in Westminster Abbey since this was written.'

Westminster Abbey is London's most illustrious church, located in the royal and political heart of the city, a short walk from the Houses of Parliament. It has a rich and ancient history, dating back to Saint Dunstan and King Edgar in the 960s, though its suspected origins are as early as the seventh century AD, or even

earlier. It is a marker of Pip's social aspirations that when he arrives in the capital in *Great Expectations*, he and Herbert Pocket go to services at the Abbey. It is built in the gothic style, with its two western towers designed by Nicholas Hawksmoor in the eighteenth century. It has been the church at which kings and queens of England and Britain have been crowned since King Harold in 1066 and, until more recently, has been the place of burial for monarchs of the realm. The interior of the church contains relics from much of its illustrious history, with elaborate tombs and effigies of monarchs and other luminaries. In *Our Mutual Friend*, when Sloppy mourns the death of Betty Higden, he prostrates himself on her simple grave and weeps over it, making a figure comparable to the abbey's effigies:

> Sloppy removed his dejected head from the church door, and took it back to the grave in the corner, and laid it down there, and wept alone. 'Not a very poor grave,' said the Reverend Frank Milvey, brushing his hand across his eyes, 'when it has that homely figure on it. Richer, I think, than it could be made by most of the sculpture in Westminster Abbey!' (*OMF*, II, III, 9)

The memorials at the abbey include those to British writers, poets and thinkers from across the centuries, dating back to Chaucer. They are gathered together in what is known as 'Poets Corner'. Dickens himself was buried here. In his writing, memorialisation at Westminster Abbey occasionally appears as shorthand for a successful life. The narrative voice in *Little Dorrit* notes that Time will show us where all the travellers on the great high road of life are headed; variously to 'the post of honour and the post of shame', to 'the mitre and the work-house', and to 'the throne and the guillotine'. The rival possible destinations include, 'to a peer's statue in Westminster Abbey and a seaman's hammock in the bosom of the deep' (*LD*, 15).

If the reference to Westminster Abbey in *Our Mutual Friend* reflects Dickens' high estimation of Sloppy's heartfelt tribute to Mrs Higden, it equally suggests the lack of enthusiasm he had for the ornate sculptures at the Abbey. Dickens strongly disliked ostentatious funerals. Mr Mould's praise of all that money can buy for Anthony Chuzzlewit in the way of funeral regalia is distasteful in Dickens' mind:

> It can give him four horses to each vehicle; it can give him velvet trappings; it can give him drivers in cloth cloaks and top-boots; it can give him the plumage of the ostrich, dyed black; it can give him any number of walking attendants, drest in the first style of funeral fashion, and carrying batons tipped with brass; it can give him a handsome tomb; it can give him a place in Westminster Abbey itself, if he choose to invest it in such a purchase. (*MC*, 19)

The 'place in Westminster Abbey itself' was an aspiration Dickens found it hard to take seriously. In *Nicholas Nickleby*, Mr Snevellici, an associate of the ridiculous Crummles troupe, sings the praises of his actor friend, Mr Glamorvey. Though not clear at first, it soon becomes apparent that Glamorvey is dead:

> 'Oh, he is dead, is he?' interrupted Nicholas.
> 'He is,' said Mr Snevellici, 'but he isn't in Westminster Abbey, more's the shame. He was a –. Well, no matter. He is gone to that bourne from whence no traveller returns. I hope he is appreciated there.' (*NN*, 30)

In his next novel, *The Old Curiosity Shop* (1840-1), Dickens parodies building memorials to the illustrious dead in his depiction of Mrs Jarley's waxworks. In fact, her exhibition seems to be a combination of a rogue's gallery and Westminster Abbey, done up in wax. The first of the 'effigies of celebrated characters' to which Nell is introduced is 'an unfortunate Maid of Honour in the Time of Queen Elizabeth, who died from pricking her finger in consequence of working upon a Sunday'. The reference is to Lady Elizabeth Russell, whose statue in Westminster Abbey shows her pointing downwards to a skull, from which the legend arose that she died from a pinprick to her forefinger. In the next chapter, with her habit of putting older waxworks to new uses, Mrs Jarley has dressed Mary Queen of Scots in a 'dark wig, white shirt-collar, and male attire', to make 'such a complete image of Lord Byron that the young ladies quite screamed when they saw it':

Miss Monflathers, however, rebuked this enthusiasm, and took occasion to reprove Mrs Jarley for not keeping her collection more select, observing that His Lordship had held certain free opinions quite incompatible with wax-work honours, and adding something about a Dean and Chapter, which Mrs Jarley did not understand. (*OCS*, 29)[7]

The oblique reference is to the 'Dean and Chapter' of Westminster Abbey, where the authorities had famously refused to allow Byron to be buried on account of his scandalous reputation. The debate had been rekindled a few years before Dickens began writing *The Old Curiosity Shop*, when it was proposed that Byron should be honoured with a statue in the Abbey instead. Dickens' friend and biographer, John Forster, responded to the discussion with a piece in his journal, *The Examiner*, in 1836.[8]

In the light of these parallels between Mrs Jarley's waxworks and the effigies and statues at Westminster Abbey, it is a heavy irony that Mr Slum should ask Mrs Jarley whether she is 'acquainted with Westminster Abbey'. He claims for himself high rank as a poet, as he tries to sell her a rhyming acrostic:

'Ask the perfumers, ask the blacking-makers, ask the hatters, ask the old lottery-office-keepers – ask any man among 'em what my poetry has done for him, and mark my words, he blesses the name of Slum. If he's an honest man, he raises his eyes to heaven, and blesses the name of Slum – mark that! You are acquainted with Westminster Abbey, Mrs Jarley?'

'Yes, surely.'

'Then upon my soul and honour, ma'am, you'll find in a certain angle of that dreary pile, called Poets' Corner, a few smaller names than Slum,' retorted that gentleman, tapping himself expressively on the forehead to imply that there was some slight quantity of brains behind it. (*OCS*, 28)

When Dickens died, on 9 June 1870, he was buried in Poets' Corner. It was an honour that he might not have appreciated had he foreseen it. His own request, as stated directly in his will and implicitly in the longer testimony of his published works, was for a simple burial:

> I emphatically direct that I be buried in an inexpensive, unostentatious and strictly private manner; that no public announcement be made of the time or place of my burial; that at the utmost not more than three plain mourning coaches be employed; and that those who attend my funeral wear no scarf, cloak, black bow, long hat-band, or other such revolting absurdity. I direct that my name be inscribed in plain English letters on my tomb, without the addition of 'Mr.' or 'Esquire.' I conjure my friends on no account to make me the subject of any monument, memorial or testimonial whatever. I rest my claims to the remembrance of my country upon my published works and to the remembrance of my friends upon their experience of me in addition thereto. [7]

A compromise was reached between the wishes of a grateful and mourning nation and the desires of Dickens himself, as he was buried, without prior announcement and in the most closely guarded and private fashion, in Westminster Abbey. A simple black tablet marks his grave in Poets' Corner and reads: 'Charles Dickens Born 7th February 1812 Died 9th June 1870'.

The day after the funeral, one newspaper reported the events of the previous morning as follows:

> At six o'clock yesterday morning the body was removed from Gadshill-place and conveyed by special train to Charing Cross. There, a plain hearse and three mourning coaches were in waiting, and so secretly was every detail arranged that the procession left the station without anyone knowing that it was the funeral of Charles Dickens. The hearse and coaches crept slowly down the Strand, along Whitehall and King-street to the Abbey door, where Dean Stanley and a few clergymen in robes awaited the arrival of the corpse. [9]

This was Dickens' final passage through London: from Charing Cross Station, down the Strand, to Trafalgar Square and Charing Cross itself, where David Copperfield once looked out dismally through the rain at the statue of King George I on horseback. There, the hearse turned down Whitehall, and proceeded on to Westminster Abbey. He was taken, for the last time, through the streets that he had traversed on so many occasions before; brought back to the city that had so constantly and characteristically fired his imagination. At 9.30 in the morning, the funeral began and Charles Dickens was buried in Poet's Corner, Westminster Abbey – a place he would not have chosen for himself, but at the heart of the city he loved.

NOTES

INTRODUCTION

1. Letter to John Forster, 30 August 1846, *Letters*, IV, p. 612.
2. Quoted in Gladys Storey, *Dickens and Daughter* (1939), p. 92.

1. LONDON SLUMS

1. Anthony S. Wohl, *The Eternal Slum: Housing and Social Policy in Victorian London* (1977); and Roy Porter, London: *A Social History* (1994), pp. 312-38.
2. J. A. Yelling, *Slums and Slum Clearance in Victorian London* (1986). And see Wohl, *The Eternal Slum*, p. 27.
3. For example, D.A. Miller, The Novel and the Police (1988).
4. John R. Reed, *Dickens' Hyperrealism* (2010), p. 17.

2. AFFLUENT LONDON

1. Quotations from the Autobiographical Fragment are taken from John Forster, *The Life of Charles Dickens* (1872–4)
2. F. H. W. Shepherd (ed.), *Survey of London: volumes 31 and 32*: St James Westminster, Part 2 (1963), pp. 138-45.

3. COACH HOUSES AND HOTELS

1. T.C. Barker and C.I. Savage, *An Economic History of Transport in Britain* (1959, repr. 2006); esp. pp. 49-52 and 125-27.
2. Stephen Inwood, *Historic London: An Explorer's Companion* (2008), p. 211.
3. Dorian Gerhold, 'Mountain, Sarah Ann (1769/70–1842)', *Oxford Dictionary of National Biography*, (2004; online edn, Jan 2008); and B.W. Matz, *The Inns and Taverns of Pickwick* (1921), pp. 35ff.
4. F. W. H. Shepherd (ed.), *Survey of London*, vol. 36 (1970), pp. 91-94.

4. AT HOME IN LONDON

1. John Forster, *The Life of Charles Dickens* (1872-4).
2. Frank Green, *London Homes of Dickens* (1928).

5. LEGAL LONDON

1. David Palfreyman, *London's Inns of Court: history, law, customs and modern purpose* (2011)

6. THE RIVER AND ITS BRIDGES

1. Chris Roberts, *Cross River Traffic: A History of London's Bridges* (2006), p. 24.
2. See Brian Cookson, *Crossing the River: the History of London's Thames River Bridges from Richmond to the Tower* (2006), p. 257.
3. Roberts, *Cross River Traffic*, p. 85.
4. J. Ewing Ritchie, *The Night Side of London* (1858), p. 10.
5. Algernon Swinburne, 'Charles Dickens', *Quarterly Review* (July 1902).

7. LONDON'S PRISONS

1. Philip Collins, *Dickens and Crime* (1964).
2. See Collins, *Dickens and Crime*, pp. 27–51.
3. Richard Byrne, *Prisons and Punishments of London* (1989), pp. 25–39.
4. Byrne, *Prisons and Punishments*, pp. 60–5.
5. Byrne, *Prisons and Punishments*, pp. 140–63.

8. LONDON'S CHURCHES

1. Elizabeth and Wayland Young, *Old London Churches* (1956), p. 25.
2. John Betjeman, *City of London Churches* (1974), p. 4.
3. Christopher Hibbert, *London's Churches* (1988), p. 18.
4. See Valentine Cunningham, 'Dickens and Christianity' in David Paroissien (ed.), *Blackwell's Companion to Charles Dickens* (2008).
5. The text is taken from volume four of Michael Slater, *Dickens's Journalism* (1994–2000).
6. The text is taken from the extract, titled 'The Heart of London', in Pete Orford (ed.), *Dickens on London* (2010)
7. See Norman Page (ed.), *The Old Curiosity Shop* (London: Penguin, 2000).
8. John Forster, *The Life of Charles Dickens* (1872–4), p. 482.
9. *Leeds Mercury*, Weds 15 June, 1870.

FURTHER READING

BIOGRAPHY

Robert Douglas-Fairhurst, *Becoming Dickens* (2011)

Michael Slater, *Dickens* (2009)

Melissa Valiska Gregory and Melisa Klimaszewski, *Brief Lives: Dickens* (2007)

LONDON

Peter Ackroyd, *London: A Biography* (2000)

Roy Porter, *London: A Social History* (1994)

Francis Shepherd, *London: A History* (1998)

DICKENS AND LONDON

Peter Ackroyd (intro), *Dickens' London: An Imaginative Vision* (1989)

Murray Baumgarten, 'Fictions of the City' in John O. Jordan (ed.),
The Cambridge Companion to Dickens (2001)

Jon Mee, 'Dickens and the City' in *The Cambridge Introduction to Charles Dickens* (2010)

F. S. Schwarzbach, *Dickens and the City* (1979)

Jeremy Tambling, *Going Astray: Dickens and London* (2009)

INDEX